D0856406

Que
Gar

~The Quotable Gardener~

Words of Wisdom from Walt Whitman,
Jane Austin, Robert Frost, Martha Stewart,
The Farmer's Almanac, and More

KATHY ISHIZUKA

McGraw-Hill

New York   San Francisco   Washington, D.C.   Auckland   Bogotá
Caracas   Lisbon   London   Madrid   Mexico City   Milan
Montreal   New Delhi   San Juan   Singapore
Sydney   Tokyo   Toronto

McGraw-Hill

*A Division of The **McGraw·Hill** Companies*

1 2 3 4 5 6 7 8 9 0   DOC/DOC   0 9 8 7 6 5 4 3 2 1 0

ISBN 0-07-136061-1

This book was set in Berkeley by Binghamton Valley Composition.
Printed and bound by R. R. Donnelley & Sons Company.

McGraw-Hill books are available at special quantity discounts to use as
premiums and sales promotions, or for use in corporate training programs.
For more information, please write to the Director of Special Sales,
Professional Publishing, McGraw-Hill, Two Penn Plaza, New York, NY
10121-2298. Or contact your local bookstore.

 This book is printed on recycled, acid-free paper containing a
minimum of 50% recycled, de-inker fiber.

 *Dedication*

For my uncle,

Henry Nishi,

who helped me plant my first garden,

And all those caring adults
who nurture the love of growing things in children.

Contents

Introduction

ASSEMBLED IN THIS VOLUME are more than 1000 quotes, personal observations, and witticisms in celebration of gardening, the love of which, proclaimed Gertrude Jekyll, "is a seed that once sown never dies."

Indeed, gardening sparks true passion among its practitioners like no other endeavor. Inherently a contemplative act, gardeners spanning time and culture have thus been inspired to set down spade and fork and hold forth on every aspect of their craft. Volumes dedicated to practical advice, personal accounts, design, and various species of plant and flower have contributed to the vast—and growing—body of gardening literature.

"What another book of gardening!," exclaimed Samuel Graveson, and that was back in 1911. Yet gardeners remain persistently curious, and, largely a literate bunch, continue to demand reading material.

The sources collected here are, like my taste in plants, rather eclectic. There are the classic garden writers: Vita Sackville-West, Louise Beebe Wilder, Reginald Farrer, Gertrude Jekyll, among others. More contemporary writers, such as Ann Lovejoy and Geoffrey B. Charlesworth, expand the perspective. Beyond the prominent names, I've sought to include the thoughts and words of gardening's rank and file. United here are famed landscape designers, learned plantsmen, and plain ol' dirt gardeners, all kin of the spade.

While many classics are included, Jekyll on color, for instance, this is not so much a volume of garden writing's greatest hits, but rather a compilation that touches on the full spectrum of the gardening experience from Anticipation, Envy, and Garden Attire to Control, Earthworms, and Garden Catalogs.

There is incredible detail (Celia Thaxter's exquisite description of the California poppy), as well as overarching themes of stewardship of the earth and the profound wonder of the life cycle. Varieties of gardens are represented (English, Fantasy, Cottage,

Vegetable), as are various types of gardeners: those who view gardening as therapy, such as Anne Nelson, who wrote "Give me valium, or give me a garden," novice gardeners, slightly bewildered and saddled with advice, yet no less impassioned, and, inexplicably, nongardeners.

Compiling this book has been pure pleasure, almost as enjoyable as gardening itself. But this stack of seed catalogs has long since started to gather dust; it's time to get outside and poke around. It's a bit early, but maybe the ground has thawed in spots to do some digging. . . .

Happy reading!

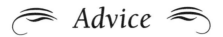 Advice

Throw all preconceived notions out the window, plant wildly, laugh at the failures, and smugly savor the successes.
> — DAN HINKLEY, *The Explorer's Garden: Rare and Unusual Plants*, 1999

This, I fear is a counsel of perfection, and I have very little hope that you will be able to follow my advice. I proffer it only knowing that it is right, which does not mean that I follow it myself.
> — VITA SACKVILLE-WEST, *Some Flowers*, 1937, on advice for cultivating verbascum

Never dig without a reason.
> — WILLIAM BRYANT LOGAN, "Dig We Might," *Garden Design* magazine April/May 1995

Plant the bean when the moon is light,
Plant the potato when the moon is dark.
Sow peas and beans in the wane of the moon,
Who soweth them sooner
He soweth too soon.
> — English country lore

Do not attempt too much.
> — THE GERMAIN FRUIT COMPANY, *1896 Catalog*

The owner of a new garden probably ought to spend his first year with his hands tied behind his back and his tools locked away in the cellar. The savings in plants and time would be remarkable. Gardeners know this, but if not restrained they forget all good sense at the sight of new soil.
> — THOMAS C. COOPER, "A Note from the Editor," *Horticulture*, July 1985

1

Don't take guff from a plant.
> ← CASSANDRA DANZ, *Mrs. Greenthumbs Plows Ahead*, 1998, on training a rose to climb

Now there are several cardinal rules to observe about making borders. The first is *observe no rules at all*. In other words, don't be afraid of muddling up the true herbaceous plants with such things as bulbs and annuals: don't be hypnotized by that very ugly and rather meaningless word herbaceous. I really prefer to call the herbaceous border the mixed border.
> ← VITA SACKVILLE-WEST, *How Does Your Garden Grow?*, 1935

Never go to a doctor whose office plants have died.
> ← ERMA BOMBECK, American humorist (1927–1996)

Many people think that, like parenting, gardening is in your bones, or they figure it's complicated or technical. If you're not experienced it's really helpful to get a basic gardening book. A good gardener also can help answer your questions and give good advice. Remember, too, that some of the best sources of information in your area are the older gardeners who know the ropes.
> ← RENEE SHEPHERD, Shepherd's Garden Seeds

A prudent man does not make the goat his gardener.
> ← Hungarian proverb

Don't wear perfume in the garden—unless you want to be pollinated by bees.
> ← ANNE RAVER, author of *Deep in the Green*, 1995

The number-one problem in gardening is putting a five-dollar plant in a fifty-cent hole.
> ← RALPH SNODSMITH, garden editor, "Good Morning, America," quoted in *Garden Smarts: A Bounty of Tips from America's Best Gardeners*, 1995

Where there is any doubt about moving a shrub or splitting up a herbaceous plant in autumn, the task should be deferred till spring. That is my official pronouncement. Don't expect me to follow it myself, because I'm also a great believer in doing a job when I want to do it, and to hell with the consequences.
— CHRISTOPHER LLOYD, *The Well-Tempered Garden*, 1997

In starting a garden, the first question, of course, is where to plant. If you are a beginner in the art, and the place is new and large, go to a good landscape gardener and let him give advice and make you a plan. But don't follow it, at least not at once, nor all at one time. Live there for a while, until you yourself begin to feel what you want, and where you want it.
— MRS. HELENA RUTHERFORD ELY, *A Woman's Hardy Garden*, 1903

Age

I am still devoted to the garden. But although an old man I am but a young gardener.
— THOMAS JEFFERSON

I am once more seated under my own vine and fig tree . . . and hope to spend the remainder of my days . . . which in the ordinary course of things (being now in my sixty-sixth year) cannot be many, in peaceful retirement; making political pursuits yield to the more rational amusement of cultivating the earth.
— GEORGE WASHINGTON, letter to J. Anderson, April 7, 1797

It is only when you start to garden—probably after fifty—that you realize something important happens every day.
— GEOFFREY B. CHARLESWORTH, *The Opinionated Gardener*, 1988

Too old to plant trees for my own gratification, I shall do it for my posterity.
— THOMAS JEFFERSON

I think it very possible for a person to become so identified with a garden that their life will be prolonged in order to prevent anyone else getting their hands on it.
— JOSEPHINE SAXTON, *Gardening Down a Rabbit Hole*, 1996

As one grows older one should grow more expert at finding beauty in unexpected places, in deserts and even in towns, in ordinary human faces and among wild weeds.
— C. C. VYVYAN, *The Old Place*, 1952

Most of us today are forced by necessity to live in towns, and sometimes we tend to dream of retirement to some cottage in the clear air of the countryside, where, we fondly imagine, our plants will grow as we wish them to grow. But gardens grow slowly, and by the time we are forced to reflect ruefully that our grey hairs are no longer premature, the time is upon us when we should enjoy the fruits of our past labours rather than look to future ones.
— ROY C. ELLIOTT, *Alpine Gardening*, 1988

By the time a man reaches forty he is either a drunkard or a gardener.
— French saying

The life so short, the craft so long to learn. This was said about literature, but it really fits gardening better. Poetry, after all, is learned extremely early, as a rule, if it is learned at all, but gardening is the province of old crocks past the age of 28.
— HENRY MITCHELL, *One Man's Garden*, 1992

One who grows does not grow old.
— TEXAS BIX BENDER, writer (1949–)

How I loath being ill! How I fight it, rebel against it, garden up to the very last moment and get up tottering to go out and replant the Violet bed.

➤ Mrs. Leslie Williams, *A Garden in the Suburbs*, 1901

In successive censuses gardeners are continuously found at the head of the tables of longevity.

➤ William Beach Thomas, *Gardens*, 1952

It has been said that a new garden is not a garden at all. And when one considers the qualities inherent in an old garden, one grown old in the service of beauty and of human delight, its amenities of shelter and shade, its glowing flower-lit stretches, its gracious softness of contour; the sense of repose, of stability, of the preserving of reverenced memories that pervades it—when one considers these things, a new garden, crude, unproved, traditionless, would seem to have no points at all in its favour.

➤ Louise Beebe Wilder, garden writer, 1924

Animals in the Garden

One day Annie decided to "tell the animals they couldn't eat here." Apparently it worked.

➤ Liza Ketchum Murrow, "Plans of Its Own," *Green Prints*, Winter 1992, 1993

Anyone who gets sentimental over a herd of deer or thinks they're cute either lives where there aren't any or else has no interest in gardening.

➤ Meg Buck, gardener, north-central New Jersey, quoted in "Cottage Garden Art," by Allen Lacy, *Horticulture*, January 1988

I am no hunter. It doesn't really matter how many legs are involved—two, four, six, eight. I don't even like to kill slugs, and they have no legs at all.

Not that I am unbloodied. I have done my share of squashing, drowning, poisoning, clubbing, and shooting. It was all, however, in self-defense. My garden was being attacked. Even pacifist vegetarians will reach for a rock when their own beans are at stake.

— ROGER B. SWAIN, "Warding off Wildlife," *Horticulture*, June 1985

I'll share the land gladly. It's only a question of numbers.

— SARA STEIN, *Noah's Garden: Restoring the Ecology of Our Own Back Yards*, 1993, on the local deer herd

Snakes of all sorts seem, from the amount of antidotes we find against them, to have been a much more common danger than they are today. Or was it that our more credulous ancestors looked more often over their shoulders to see if Eden's despoiler was silently writhing up on them? We are reminded of the necessity of always keeping a large radish handy with which to smash a snake. The plant drago's head (*dracocephalum*) now a charming addition to the garden border, has the added advantage that no serpent will go near anyone who carries it.

— DOROTHY JACOB, *A Witch's Guide to Gardening*, 1964

Distinguishing animals from plants is easy if you're a gardener: plants remain rooted in one place, while animals come under, over, or through any fence intended to exclude them.

— ROGER B. SWAIN, *Earthly Pleasures*, 1981

The toad, without which no garden would be complete.

— CHARLES DUDLEY WARNER, *My Summer in a Garden*, 1870

Rats with antlers.

— JOHN MCPHEE, American writer, on voracious deer, (1931–)

Even more dreadful than the dreadful passer-by is the London dog. The combination of a dog and owner is a law unto itself, as I realised when I watched a dog-owner hold open my gate so that her deformed pooch could direct his streaming ammoniac jet into the smiling faces of my auriculas.

— GERMAINE GREER (1939–)

Cats and plants look wonderful on postcards. In real life cats pee on plants and kill them. Try to retrain your cat to use a cat-tray in a garden shed. . . . In my experience nothing else will work except a large hungry cat-hating dog, and these dig holes in your garden.

— JOSEPHINE SAXTON, *Gardening Down a Rabbit Hole*, 1996

The Lord seems to have a role for everything – weeds, early frost, drought, even Japanese beetles – and I understand that. But pocket gophers are something else: they must be an invention of the devil.

— RICHARD C. DAVIDS, *Garden Wizardry*, 1976

"Trap wild animals and release them far away," says one catalog. Far away? *Where* is far away?

— GENE LOGSDON, "Pests, Plants or People?," *Garden Prints*,
   Spring 1998

I grew vegetables with impunity until the day the broccoli disappeared. I waited and watched and discovered that that fat, short-legged animal had learned to climb the fence, swarming over it as swiftly as a veteran of an obstacle course.

— ROGER B. SWAIN, *Earthly Pleasures*, 1981

Sat 28 May 1825
Found the old Frog in my garden that had been there this 4 years. I know it by a mark which it received from my spade 4 years ago. . . . I am glad to see it has recovered in Winter it gets into some straw in a corner of the garden and never ventures out till the beginning of May when it hides among the flowers and keeps its old bed never venturing further up the garden.

— JOHN CLARE, *Journal*, 1824–1825

⪡ Annuals/Perennials ⪢

Plants that flower, set seed and die within a single season, they can perform prodigies in their brief lives. A morning glory will throw a blue mantle over a small building in no time, tithoniums and castor plants make hedges tall as a man by midsummer.

— ELEANOR PERÉNYI, *Green Thoughts*, 1981

Gardeners are generous people and perennials, which grow and multiply, help foster these generous instincts.

— DAVID SCHEID, *Taylor's Guide to Gardening: Perennials*, 1984

Planting is one of my great amusements, and even of those things which can only be for posterity, for a septuagenary has no right to count on anything beyond annuals.

— THOMAS JEFFERSON

Of all the perennials I grow that show tendencies to transcience, columbines are the most fascinating and ingratiating for in their disappearance they also tend to leave other, often quite different, columbines in their place.

— ALLEN LACY, *Home Ground: A Gardener's Miscellany*, 1984

I demand that the plant be able to support itself without staking, not appear sloppy or rank at any time, and not require extensive management like spraying, pinching, or pruning. Tasks like deadheading will produce dead heads.

— JEROME MALITZ, *Personal Landscapes*, 1984, on perennials

I must sound two warning notes [about annuals]. The first is that seed catalogues are intended to beguile and enchant and make intricate seem straight, and their descriptions and illustrations can be misleading, particularly about colour. The second is that many annuals have passed through the hands of demented hybridists and have surfaced in grotesque forms, with monstrous heads or extra limbs and with every drop of natural grace and simplicity drained from them.

➤ STEPHEN LACEY, *The Startling Jungle: Colour and Scent in the Romantic Garden*, 1990

They use perennials like annual bedding plants, taking them up every year and cutting them in half and resetting them. This is the highest-maintenance form of gardening there can be, but they can't wait for the four years for the plants to grow together.

➤ FRED McGOURTY, Connecticut nursery worker, on impatient novices who desire an instant garden, quoted in "Paradise Found," *TIME* magazine, June 20, 1988

Sooner or later one has to make up one's mind as to whether half-hardy annuals are worth growing or not. They certainly take up a lot of time, and once the frost has cut them down they are gone for ever, and all our labour with them . . .

➤ VITA SACKVILLE-WEST, *Some Flowers*, 1937

He wondered if I had heard of perennials. Of course I had heard of perennials. Every Sunday the news in the papers waited until I had finished the garden sections; I subscribed to four garden magazines; I now owned six garden books—how could I have kept from hearing about perennials? But that I knew nothing about growing perennials was obvious to Mr. Platt.

➤ AMOS PETTINGILL, horticulturist (1900–1981)

Anticipation

One of the most delightful things about a garden is the anticipation it provides.

➤ W. E. JOHNS, *My Garden*, 1937

The first pleasant thing about a garden in this latitude is that you never know when to set it going. If you want anything to come to maturity early, you must start it in a hot-house. If you put it out early, the chances are all in favor of getting it nipped with frost; for the thermometer will be 90° one day, and go below 32° the night of the day following. And, if you do not set out plants or sow seeds early, you fret continually; knowing that your vegetables will be late, and that, while Jones has early peas you will be watching your slow-forming pods. This will keep you in a state of mind.

— CHARLES DUDLEY WARNER, *My Summer in a Garden*, 1870

The way we are enticed into a garden and encouraged to pursue its experience to the end is like the plot of a novel. It is the thread on which the whole story unfolds.

— JOE ECK, *Elements of Garden Design*, 1996

From May on, I can hardly wait to get up to see what has happened overnight, for one of the pleasures of a garden is that something is always happening; it is not static, even for a day. I go out by six-thirty and sometimes earlier, still in my pajamas and a wrapper, to take a look around before breakfast.

— MAY SARTON, *Plant Dreaming Deep*, 1968

 *Architecture*

Architecture is the mother art of gardens, not because a garden needs to be (or should be) cluttered with architectural gewgaws, but because the stuff of architecture—the tensions between different volumes, the fall of light and dark, the rhythms of texture – is the essence of a garden.

— HENRY MITCHELL, *One Man's Garden*, 1992

We enjoy as a lawful luxury their easy windings and purposed prolongation. Yet even these should not be wholly capricious. Let there be at least some reason for every turn—some compensatory attraction for every delay.

— HENRY CLEAVELAND, *Village and Farm Cottages*, 1856, on the subject of garden paths

The works of a person that builds begin immediately to decay; while those of him who plants begin directly to improve. In this, planting promises a more lasting pleasure than building.

— WILLIAM SHENSTONE, English poet (1714–1763)

This somewhat recent development in landscape design has been a great setback both to gardening and to architecture since its inception. The original purpose was to conceal the results of bad building, faulty architecture and poor site planning by slapping an assortment of evergreens up against the foundations of a new house. Around a trailer, where they are best employed, they can lend a spurious air of permanence; they can also make a beautiful old country home look like a trailer. These plantings are now an almost universal landscape cliché—homeowners don't plant them because they like the plants; as gardeners find themselves pruning them several times a year, they like them less and less. And most old homes have less than no need of an evergreen fringe around their lower level.

— PATRICIA THORPE, *The American Weekend Gardener*, 1988, on meatball-shaped evergreens called a foundation planting

I failed to look up and out at shapes and heights of trees, shrubs, and structures that give the garden form. My eyes were always at flower level. A visiting friend, looking at the front of my house, started waving her hands around in the air, trying to show me how the house needed framing with plants. . . . I had never considered shapes, lines or flow to be a part of gardening.

— BARBARA ASHMUN, *The Garden Design Primer*, 1994

The best advice I ever received about gardening was to plant the "bones" early and not to worry about the details; they could adapt and change as inclination and experience allowed.

➤ MONTAGU DON, *The Sensuous Garden*, 1997

Everybody thinks architecture in a garden is anathema today. On the contrary, geometry gives pure pleasure.

➤ PATRICK CHASSE, garden designer, quoted in *Breaking Ground: Portraits of Ten Garden Designers* by Page Dickey, 1997

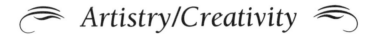

Artistry/Creativity

I notice that it is only when my mother is working in her flowers that she is radiant; almost to the point of being invisible—except as Creator: hand and eye. She is involved in work her soul must have. Ordering the universe in the image of her personal conception of Beauty.

➤ ALICE WALKER, *In Search of Our Mother's Gardens*, 1983

Adam and Eve were born in the garden, and gardens are still where people go to renew themselves by creation.

➤ CAROL WILLIAMS, *Bringing a Garden to Life*, 1998

Nobody wants a garden exactly like anybody else's garden. Never will it happen, never in the world, so long as human vanity lasts. A garden is one place in the world where the urge can be indulged ad lib. There are no overseers to frown, no motorcycle police to ride up alongside and say "Pull over to the curb! Where do you think you are going with all those blazing red geraniums?"

➤ LEONARD H. ROBBINS, *Cure It with a Garden*, 1933

Since I have been here, the deserted garden, planted with large pines beneath which grows the grass, tall and unkempt and mixed with various weeds, has sufficed for my work and I have not yet gone outside. . . . By staying here, the doctor will naturally be better able to see what is wrong and will be, I hope, more reassured as to my being allowed to paint.

— VINCENT VAN GOGH (1853–1890)

Garden art has all the advantage over painted art, for it is not static. Gardening calls for an artist's eye for color and form coupled with the musician's sense of developing a theme over time—something the visual artist can't do.

— KEVIN NICOLAY, **botanical artist, quoted in** *Horticulture*, **January 1990**

Any art is long, and the gardening art is one of the longest.

— LEONARD H. ROBBINS, *Cure It with a Garden*, 1933

For planting ground is painting a landscape with living things and I hold that good gardening takes rank within the bounds of the fine arts, so I hold that to plant well needs an artist of no mean capacity.

— GERTRUDE JEKYLL, *Wood and Garden*, 1899

A leaf or a twig, the fell of a stone step under one's tread, a trickle of water, the musky smell of a cyclamen plant set in a pot that you have but to tap to know from the sound whether it needs watering or not, such transient impressions as these can open a door and set in motion a whole world of garden pictures.

— RUSSELL PAGE, *Education of a Gardener*, 1962

The best garden should be a personal expression. It shouldn't matter if the owner of a gas station hasn't studied the principles of Gertrude Jekyll. As I drive into my local service station, I enjoy seeing those discarded radials potted up with impatiens. They take the edge off the bleakness of an asphalt landscape.

— MICHAEL POLLAN, *The New York Times*, September 25, 1994

All gardening is landscape-painting.
— ALEXANDER POPE (1688–1784)

Garden making is a creative work. . . . It is a personal expression of self, an individual conception of beauty. I should as soon think of asking a secretary to write my book, or the cook to assist in a water color painting, as to permit a gardener to plant or dig among my flowers.
— HANNA RION, *Let's Make a Flower Garden*, 1912

In his garden every man may be his own artist without apology or explanation.
— LOUISE BEEBE WILDER, *Color in My Garden*, 1990

I have never had so many good ideas day after day as when I worked in the garden.
— JOHN ERSKINE, (1879–1951)

Your garden may be clipped, neo-classical, random cottage style, modern high-tech, or some intensely personal vision of Byzantium that nobody, anywhere, has ever thought of before. Do not let anyone tread upon these dreams.
— ANNA PAVORD, *The Border Book*, 1994

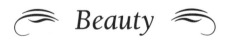 *Beauty*

No synonym for God is so perfect as Beauty! Whether as seen carving the lines of the mountains with glaciers, or gathering matter into stars, or planning the movements of water, or gardening-still all is Beauty!
— JOHN MUIR, quoted in *The Wilderness World of John Muir* by Edwin Way Teale, 1954

You do not need to know anything about a plant to know that it is beautiful.

    ← Montagu Don, *The Sensuous Garden*, 1997

In order to comprehend the beauty of a Japanese garden, it is necessary to understand—or at least to learn to understand—the beauty of stones. Not of stones quarried by the hand of man, but of stones shaped by nature only. Until you can feel, and keenly feel, that stones have character, that stones have tones and values, the whole artistic meaning of a Japanese garden cannot be revealed to you.

    ← Lafcadio Hearn, *Glimpses of Unfamiliar Japan*, 1894

There is no such thing as an ugly garden—gardens, like babies, are all beautiful to their parents.

    ← Ken Druse, *The Collector's Garden*, 1996

The beauty of a plant lies not just in the vision of a moment, but in what it was and will be, from seed to leaf, from senescence to decay—and renewal.

    ← Derek Toms, "An Essayist in the Garden: A Farewell to Gardening?" *Hortus*, Spring 1995

I like making beauty that isn't sweet. It is a hard and firm beauty.

    ← Robert Dash, painter, quoted in "Paradise Found," *TIME* magazine, June 20, 1988

My flower garden has a purpose, although it may not be as obvious as the purpose of a staple gun. It is beautiful.

    ← Cassandra Danz, *Mrs. Greenthumbs*, 1993

As I hold the flower in my hand and think of trying to describe it, I realize how poor a creature I am, how impotent are words in the presence of such perfection. It is held upright upon a straight and polished stem, its petals curving upward and outward into the cup of light, pure gold with a lustrous satin sheen; a rich orange is painted on the gold drawn in infinitely fine lines to a point in the center of the edge of each petal so that the effect is that of a diamond of flame in a cup of gold.

━ CELIA THAXTER, *An Island Garden* 1895, describing the California poppy

The truth is that flower breeders tend to be concerned with the more and more, while they should be concerned with the better and more beautiful.

━ DAVID AUSTIN, *Old Roses and English Roses*, 1993, on modern rose breeding

Of all things made by man for his pleasure, a flower garden has least business to be ugly, barren or stereotyped, because in it we may have the fairest of the earth's children in a living, ever-changeful state, and not, as in other arts, mere representation of them.

━ WILLIAM ROBINSON, garden designer (1838–1935)

Just think of the beauty that is available in leaves alone.

━ GRAHAM STUART THOMAS, *Perennial Garden Plants*, 1976

 *Bees and Butterflies*

Nothing is like a soul as a bee. It goes from flower to flower as a soul from star to star, and it gathers honey as a soul gathers light.

━ VICTOR HUGO, *Les Misérables*, 1862

We often complain about the uniformity of shippable but dull grocery-store produce and yet tolerate the same look in a garden: huge cabbages of 'Peace' roses, impossibly pink dinner-plates of dahlias. A few holes in some leaves here and there, more bees and beetles, a stray bird's nest, and even butterflies over the veronica. . . . These things can add to a garden's beauty in the same way that they embellish the still lifes of the Dutch masters.

— ROSALIE H. DAVIS, "Butterfly Gardening," *Horticulture*, June 1989

The bees like plum-blossoms, and so do I. They smell exactly like cherry Lifesavers taste.

— SUE HUBBELL, *A Book of Bees*, 1988

Butterflies add another dimension in the garden for they are like dream flowers—childhood dreams—which have broken loose from their stalk and escaped into the sunshine. Air and angels. This is the way I look upon their presence—not as a professional entomologist, any more than I look upon roses as a botanist might.

— MIRIAM ROTHSCHILD, *The Butterfly Gardener*, 1983

The hum of bees is the voice of the garden.

— ELIZABETH LAWRENCE, *Through the Garden Gate*, 1990

How doth the little busy bee
Improve each shining hour,
And gather honey all the day
From every opening flower!

— ISAAC WATTS, "Against Idleness and Mischief," *Divine Songs for Children*, 1715

 Birds

We charge every man with positive dishonesty who drives birds from his garden at fruit time. The fruit is theirs as well as yours. They took care of it as much as you did. If they had not eaten egg, worm and bug, your fruit would have been pierced and ruined. They only come for wages. No honest man will cheat a bird of his spring and summer's work.

— HENRY WARD BEECHER, American clergyman (1813–1887)

I once had a sparrow alight upon my shoulder for a moment while I was hoeing in a village garden, and I felt that I was more distinguished by that circumstance than I should have been by any epaulet I could have worn.

— HENRY DAVID THOREAU, *Winter Visitors, Walden,* 1854

The most approving, expectant and appreciative of small creatures, and one of the few which never seems to have learnt that man is the Enemy. The presence of a robin, sitting with his head on one side on a fence-post three feet away from you while you are digging on a fine autumn day, waiting for the next clod to be turned over so that he can nip down and see what you've provided for him creates a feeling of relationship between man and bird which is normally reserved for geniuses like Konrad Lorenz.

— HUGH POPHAM, *Gentlemen Peasants: A Gardener's ABC,* 1968

I have also begun to fear for birds, and in recent years taken steps to encourage them. I removed the scarecrow from the vegetable garden, which I was glad to do anyway. Dressed in my cast-off clothes, this figure had become an increasingly derelict version of myself, and though it didn't really keep off the birds, it had begun to frighten me to death.

— ELEANOR PERÉNYI, American author (1918–)

When monardas come into bloom they bring the hummingbirds careening into the new garden, where masses of "Cambridge Scarlet" and "Gardenview Scarlet" bee balm stand against giant, brilliant orange lilies. Add several gleaming iridescent green and red hummingbirds to the floral composition, and you'll stand marveling at what God, and you, have wrought.

— ELISABETH SHELDON, *The Flamboyant Garden*, 1997

 *Bonsai*

A bonsai is a wondrous thing: in less space than a man can encompass with his arms, it can suggest a whole world of venerable old trees. A single plant may embody in itself the majesty of a great forest; alone, it can suggest the mysterious depths of distant mountain valleys. Gazing at it, one forgets that it is a small, manmade "nature" and senses oneself transported to the mysterious realm of great Nature itself.

— HIDEO ARAGAKI, *Classic Bonsai of Japan*, 1990

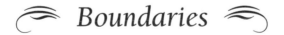 *Boundaries*

A garden without a fence is like a dog without a tail.

— Moroccan proverb

I like neighbors and I like chickens; but I do not think they ought to be united near a garden. Neighbors' hens in your garden are an annoyance. Even if they did not scratch up the corn, and peck the strawberries, and eat the tomatoes, it is not pleasant to see them straddling about in their jerky, high-stepping, speculative manner, picking inquisitively here and there. It is of no use to tell the neighbor that his hens eat your tomatoes: it makes no impression on him, for the tomatoes are not his. The best way is to casually remark to him that he has a fine lot of chickens, pretty well grown, and that you like spring chickens broiled. He will take them away at once.

➳ CHARLES DUDLEY WARNER, *My Summer in a Garden*, 1870

No garden, great or small, should be seen all at one glance; barriers of some kind must be maintained or introduced to give some elements of surprise and secrecy to a garden tour.

➳ PENELOPE HOBHOUSE, *The Country Gardener*, 1976

Love your neighbour, yet pull not down your hedge.

➳ GEORGE HERBERT, English poet, (1593–1633)

The roses had given up their annual struggle to keep things cheerful and now hemmed in Mr. Rowse's path with thorns.

➳ FAY WELDON, English novelist (1931–)

If your garden is all that stands between your domestic hearth and a tourist-junkie-drunk-and-football-fan-infested street, you need to cultivate plants which actually inflict pain upon the unwary interloper. A large holly-bush will defend itself adequately against a toppling drunk or swooning dope-fiend, but as it is very slow-growing, it may be more rewarding to concentrate upon the more intractable roses.

➳ GERMAINE GREER, (1939–)

Americans must be far more brotherly-hearted than we are for they do not seem to mind being overlooked. They have no sense of private enclosure. They never plant hedges to cut themselves off from the gaze of the passerby, nor do they plant hedges between their own garden and their neighbors. All is open. Walk in, walk in! they seem to say, in cordial invitation.

➳ VITA SACKVILLE-WEST, garden writer (1892–1962)

One should learn also to enjoy the neighbor's garden, however small; the roses struggling over the fence, the scent of lilacs drifting across the road.

— HENRY VAN DYKE, American clergyman (1852–1933)

 *Buds*

You must stand still; and then you will see open lips and furtive glances, tender fingers, and raised arms, the fragility of a baby, and the rebellious outburst of the will to live; and then you will hear the infinite march of buds faintly roaring.

— KAREL CAPEK, "The March of Buds," *The Gardener's Year*, 1929

A Rose is sweeter in the bud than full blown.

— JOHN LYLY, English dramatist and author (1554–1606)

Nature mothers these frail little wall plants in their limited nursery throughout the winter months. Before Spring has fully displayed its handiwork in the garden these rock plants venture to send out new buds that veil the gray rocks with all the colours of the Dawn.

— HUGH FINDLAY, *Garden Making and Keeping*, 1932

A lovely being, scarcely formed or moulded,
A rose with all its sweetest leaves yet folded.

— LORD BYRON (GEORGE GORDON), *Don Juan*, canto 15 st. 89,
1819–1824

Answering to their names
Out of the soil the buds come,
The silent detonations of power
Wielded without sin.

— R. S. THOMAS, *A Book of Gardens*, 1963

Bulbs

In spring the first snowdrops pierce the icy soil with dainty white flowers wrapped in protective membranes. They are more charming in combination with the first flowers on hellebores than isolated in lonely splendor. In summer, lilies, no matter how regal, are finer when woven through a tapestry of other flowers. It is the harmonious use of plants in combination that creates a garden rather than a mere collection.

— JUDY GLATTSTEIN, *The American Gardener's World of Bulbs*, 1994

I like to think of them [bulbs] as anything which a nurseryman can dig up, dry off and post in a packet; a very unscientific definition but more or less true.

— BRIAN MATHEW, *Growing Bulbs: The Complete Practical Guide*, 1997

Gardening has a magical quality when you are child. You plant little dry brown bulbs in the fall, and while they are sleeping through the winter you almost forget about them. But in the spring they remember to come up as bright yellow and purple crocuses.

— BARBARA DAMROSCH, *Theme Gardens*, 1982

Anyone who has a bulb has spring.

— ANONYMOUS

⪊ *Challenge/Failure* ⪉

The whole essence of joy, if one loves the garden, is to struggle to the ideal beauty in one's own pig-headed way.

⟶ Marion Cran, *The Garden of Ignorance*, 1913

I think about retreating as often as I think about dying. When something is inevitable, you do what you have to do. It isn't necessarily pleasant. The problem of giving up even part of a garden is a little like asking "would I want to go on living if . . ." The answer is usually yes. Especially if you put in a whole bunch of provisos. But *in extremis* the answer would be no. And with a garden, too, if all work had lost its savor and the nephew moved away, you might want to hire a team of upkeep types to run around once a week. A tear falls at this gloomy thought. I shall hope to die digging.

⟶ Geoffrey B. Charlesworth, *The Opinionated Gardener*, 1988

To many gardeners the most desirable plants are in the touch-and-go zone, not because they are in any objective sense more beautiful than more rugged plants, but because each one is an illegitimate addition to his repertoire, holding all the charm of the chancy and forbidden.

⟶ Hugh Johnson, *Hugh Johnson's Gardening Companion*, 1996

My garden is more of a problem than most, because I expect it to be beautiful every day of the year, and at the same time it must make room for plants that are new to me and may grow poorly or not at all.

⟶ Elizabeth Lawrence, *Through the Garden Gate*, 1990

The man around the corner keeps experimenting with new flowers every year, and now has quite an extensive list of things he can't grow.

⟶ William Vaughn, **English poet (1577–1641)**

Designing a garden is the beginning of a series of mistakes.

— MIRABEL OSLER, quoted in *Garden Design* magazine, Spring 1988

Making mistakes is one of the most important tools in garden making. If we want to do something different, to get beyond the safe and obvious, we have to be willing to be wrong sometimes. The trick is to know that mistakes don't matter, they're part of the learning process. Daring to be wrong is how great gardens get made.

— MARCO STUFANO, director of Horticulture, Wave Hill, New York, quoted in *The American Mixed Border* by Ann Lovejoy, 1993

. . . while proficiency is admirable, even the disasters entertain.

— AURELIA SCOTT, "A Gardener's Progress," *Garden Design* magazine July/August 1993

After killing off a number of plants inadvertently, it may be hard to face horticultural euthanasia. It is easy to stall: maybe this year will be milder, maybe it needs more time to settle in. . . . But the misfortune of these mistakes goes beyond a small blot on your landscape. These sad relics are the lessons you are refusing to learn.

— PATRICIA THORPE, *Growing Pains: Time and Change in the Garden*, 1994

Our final lesson is that now we keep our heads. Plants that die after three repeats are banished.

— MIRABEL OSLER, quoted in *Garden Design* magazine, Spring 1988

He planned for, and planted, rare subjects that he might never see mature—just as well perhaps, disappointments were the only certainty he acknowledged.

— MOLLY KEANE, *Time after Time*, 1983

There is something odd in the soul of gardeners, who thrive on all the strife and worry that accompany a hobby whose goal is to produce beauty. Anyone who tells you that gardening is soothing, is either lying or old and mellow. After all, it's such a problem ridden area that the federal government subsidizes a health department and infirmary—the Cooperative Extension Service—to care for those wounded in the line of duty.

— MARTHA SMITH, *Beds I Have Known: Confessions of a Passionate Amateur Gardener*, 1990

You must not, any of you, be surprised if you have moments in your gardening life of such profound depression and disappointment that you will almost wish you had been content to leave everything alone and have no garden at all.

— MRS. C. W. EARLE, *Pot-Pourri from a Surrey Garden*, 1897

I know no summer-flowering shrub as beautiful as the Hydrangea *paniculata grandiflora*. I have tried over and over again to grow it, but it does badly and then dies.

— MRS. C. W. EARLE, *Pot-Pourri from a Surrey Garden*, 1897

Acid-loving plants are often blue-flowered. Most of them will not survive in limey soil. It is a waste of time and money to try, but you will.

— JOSEPHINE SAXTON, *Gardening Down a Rabbit Hole*, 1996

Yes, gardening gives one back a sense of proportion about everything except itself. What a relief it was to me when I read that Vita Sackville-West kept a pile of metal labels in a shed at Sissinghurst as proof of all the experiments that had failed!

— MAY SARTON, *Plant Dreaming Deep*, 1968

A garden is always a series of losses set against a few triumphs, like life itself.

— MAY SARTON, *At Seventy*, 1984

Buried in my mind, like a seed waiting to break from dormancy, was the thought of a big border in sun, and with the garden expansion that idea found its moment. I visualised the drama of sword shapes and thistle shapes, metallic and angular. I knew such plants come from dry climates, but that did not stop me from coveting them.

— JO MUNRO "A Sense of Place," *Hortus*, Autumn 1999

 *Children/Childhood*

There is a garden in every childhood, an enchanted place where colors are brighter, the air softer, and the morning more fragrant than ever again.

— ELIZABETH LAWRENCE, garden writer (1904–1985)

A child examines a flower not so much for what it is, as for what . . . it might be. The furry leaves of the Stachys lanata are rabbits ears, antirrhinums are bunny's mouths, foxgloves are thimbles. That sweetpeas are babies bonnets must be obvious to anyone . . .

— LESLEY GORDON, *Green Magic*, 1977

Strange as it may sound, I have found the best preparation for fatherhood has been gardening. It takes time. Rewards are slow in coming. There is no control, only influence. Seedlings strive to develop their potential without my efforts. There is a pattern to development that is predictable in form but individual in detail and that unfolds at its own pace, whatever I may wish. Every day brings new surprises.

— NIGEL GODDARD, on Father's Day, *The New York Times*, June 26, 1994

What I do know is that few satisfactions match having grown-up children who obviously share my belief that digging in the earth has, since Eden, been the best way of staying out of trouble and meanwhile experiencing sensual delights that beggar my powers of description.

━ ALLEN LACY, garden writer (1935–)

Who, that was blessed with parents that indulged themselves, and children with a flower garden, can forget the happy innocent hours spent in its cultivation! O! who can forget those days, when to announce the appearance of a bud, or the coloring of a tulip, or the opening of a rose, or the perfection of a full-blown peony, was glory enough for one morning.

━ JOSEPH BRECK, *New Book of Flowers*, 1866

I am inclined to think that the flowers we most love are those we knew when we were very young, when our senses were most acute to color and to smell, and our natures most lyrical.

━ DOROTHY THOMPSON, *The Courage to Be Happy*, 1957

When I was a little girl, my mother took great pains to interest me in . . . planting a garden.

━ ELIZABETH LAWRENCE, garden writer, (1904–1985)

Farm children have little love for Nature and are surprisingly ig-norant about wildflowers save a few varieties. The child who is garden bred has a happier start in life, a greater love and knowledge of Nature.

━ ALICE MORSE EARLE, garden writer (1851–1911)

Give children a spot in the garden that is theirs, where they have dominion. . . . Instilling in a child love and reverence for life and the earth means giving the child love and respect. Buying rainforest t-shirts is all well and good, but the child needs to know he or she is connected to the earth wherever that child is, even indoors with plants in a city apartment.

━ JUDITH HANDELSMAN, *Growing Myself*, 1996

"Look Mommy,"he whispered. "The butterflies are dancing." At that moment, inside my soul somewhere, all the tumblers fell into place.

— KATHY STORFER, "A Dig in the Dirt," *Green Prints* Spring 1997

O geraniums, and yours, O foxgloves,
springing up amidst the coppice,
that gave my childish cheeks their rosy warmth.

— COLETTE, *Sido*, 1922

One summer day,
I chanced to stray
To a garden of flowers blooming wild.
It took me once more
To the dear days of yore
And a spot that I loved as a child.

— COLE PORTER, "An Old Fashioned Garden," 1919

All through the days of childhood the garden is our fairy-ground of sweet enchantment and innocent wonder.

— E. V. BOYLE, *Seven Gardens and a Palace*, 1900

I think of warm, barefoot days when four sets of tiny toes trampled fresh-plowed ground, leaving indelible footprints on my heart and in my memory.

— JEAN LAFFERTY, "Turning Up Memories," *Green Prints*, Spring 1999

One day Scott brought home a thistle. "That's a weed," I said. "So? You said this was a garden for kids. I'm a kid. I'll plant it if I want."

— ERICA SANDERS, "A Garden Is to Grow," *Green Prints*, Autumn 1990

There must be amusements in every family. Children observe and follow their parents in almost everything. How much better, during a long and dreary winter, for daughters, and even sons, to assist, or attend, their mother, in a green-house, than to be seated with her at cards, or, in the blubberings over a stupid novel, or at any other amusement that can possibly be conceived!

— WILLIAM COBBETT, *The English Gardener*, 1829

City Gardens

Indeed it is remarkable how nature goes on existing unofficially, as it were, in the very heart of London.

— GEORGE ORWELL, **English novelist (1903–1950)**

The innocent must be counseled before tasting of the pleasures a city garden brings: a refuge from a world of troubles, an oasis where waters truly heal.

— LINDA YANG, *The City Gardener's Handbook*, 1990

Although it is true that near London plants in general will not thrive so well as in a purer air, and that people in the country have usually some portion of ground to make a garden of, yet such persons as are condemned to a town life will do well to obtain whatever substitute for a garden may be in their power; for there is confessedly no greater folly than that of refusing all pleasure, because we cannot have all we desire.

— ELIZABETH KENT, 1831

I've lived here 20 years, and we never used to talk to people on the street. I've never been outgoing. But the garden has changed my place in life.

— SANDRA KLEINMAN, **who helps tend a community garden in New York's "Alphabet City," quoted in "Paradise Found,"** TIME *magazine*, **June 20, 1988**

City gardeners must be a determined group. In order to make a community garden out of a vacant or abandoned lot, they must tackle bureaucracy, red tape, rubble, and garbage before beginning to plant.

➤ LYNDEN B. MILLER, Perennial Plant Association Symposium, 1986

The overall character of a town garden is determined by two basic principles: it is either an extension of the rooms of the house . . . or an illusion of country come to town . . .

➤ SUSAN JELLICOE, *Town Gardens to Live In*, 1977

Even though our house was on the edge of a rough neighborhood, each act of vandalism seemed to be balanced by one of anonymous generosity. Pots of lilies and spent florist's azaleas were left on the porch, and once we found several sacks of manure with an anonymous note reading, "For the roses."

➤ ANN LOVEJOY, *The American Mixed Border*, 1993

Flowers in a city are like lipstick on a woman—it just makes you look better to have a little color.

➤ LADY BIRD JOHNSON, quoted in *TIME* magazine, May 9, 1988

Over the years, in sundry overheated, undersunned New York City caves, I have killed scores of gardenias. After each gardeniacide I would wait a decent interval and then, ever the Sisyphean gardener, buy another. I would cart it home in full bud, Proustily expectant of the first redolent waft of bensyl-acetate-styrolyl acetate-linalool-linalyl acetate-terpineol-methylanthranilate—Gardenia Absolute. Within days, the fat green buds would yellow, brown off and drop off: The gardenia would drop dead.

➤ PATTI HAGEN, "For Happy Gardenias, Drink More Coffee," *The Wall Street Journal*, September 13, 1990

Even the tiniest garden, a few rods, maybe, between the stares of buildings is ennobled by the planting of trees. Otherwise the walls lean in, and there is nothing to lift your garden above the level of the eye and hide the peering windows, the lavatory and the clothes line of the house next door.

— MURIEL STUART, *Fool's Garden*, 1936

It's a special treat to walk by a colorful front yard on a busy street, or to peek through a gate and enjoy a glimpse of a carefully tended patio or balcony terrace. There's nothing quite like a flourishing garden in a sea of concrete and glass.

— JANE G. PEPPER, president, Pennsylvania Horticultural Society, quoted in *The City Gardener's Handbook* by Linda Yang, 1990

 *Collectors*

Always try to grow in your garden some plant or plants out of the ordinary, something your neighbors never attempted. For you can receive no greater flattery than to have a gardener of equal intelligence stand before your plants and ask, "What is that?"

— RICHARDSON WRIGHT, *Another Gardener's Bed-Book*, 1933

One does not collect alpine plants as one collects stamps or cigarette cards; each plant is an individual. It may succeed brilliantly in your garden, and fail lamentably in your neighbour's, but the chances are that it will succeed—given the right growing conditions and the right setting.

— ROY C. ELLIOTT, *Alpine Gardening*, 1988

If it is rare, we want it. If it is tiny and impossible to grow, we've got to have it. If it's brown, looks dead, and has black flowers, we'll kill for it. We are collectors and little will stand in the way of bagging our quarry.

➛ KEN DRUSE, *The Collector's Garden*, 1996

I tell my neighbors, if I'm missing, you know he's put me in the bog with those plants. Sometimes I feel like I live in the "Little Shop of Horrors."

➛ **ALISON PHILLIP, whose husband built two faux swamps and filled them with his $5000 collection of carnivorous plants, quoted in "The Garden of Eatin'," by Eileen White Read,** *The Wall Street Journal*, **October 29, 1999**

The tendency to make a garden a curiosity shop is another hard one to resist. Many such gardens are enthusiastically exhibited every year. "These are our delphiniums; next our painted daisies Give a look at our Oriental poppies. Here are our Japanese irises, and we now pass on to our daylilies." Each object in the garden is admirable in itself. The sad fact remains that the garden, with all its treasures, is junky.

➛ LEONARD H. ROBBINS, *Cure It with a Garden*, 1933

The more I think about it, the stranger the idea of gardening be-comes. Not just the more blatant aberrations we have created, such as plants herded into prison exercise yards (euphemistically known as "parterres"), shrubs butchered into truncated cones, colour-coordinated borders, or freaks painstakingly bred for the sake of a reflexed petal or picotee. Most gardens are a trauma (in the path-ological sense). . . . But above all, I am puzzled as to why we have this need to surround ourselves with arbitrary and eclectic plant collections.

➛ DEREK TOMS, "An Essayist in the Garden: A Farewell to Garden-ing?" *Hortus*, Spring 1995.

Miniature everythings are in great demand. People have less space—and more interest.

— KLAUS NEUBNER, "Park's Seeds," *Newsweek* magazine, June 11, 1979

Trees are my 87th collection. As with all our collections, our goal is to put together the best kind of each kind in the world.

— LOUIS MEIZEL, New York art dealer, who has spent $100,000, thus far, on his collection, quoted in "Paradise Found," *TIME* magazine, June 20, 1988

 *Color*

The successful use of color in a garden involves not just the contribution of the artist's eye for color, but also the more practical skills of a plantsperson, agronomist, pest-control specialist, farmer, gardener, landscape designer, garden designer, and irrigation specialist.

— JEFF COX, *Creating a Garden for the Senses*, 1993

It is a curious thing that people will sometimes spoil some garden project for the sake of a word. For instance, a blue garden, for beauty's sake, may be hungering for a group of white Lilies, or for something of palest lemon-yellow, but it is not allowed to have it because it is called the blue garden, and there must be no flowers in it but blue flowers. I can see no sense in this; it seems to me like fetters foolishly self-imposed, Surely the business of the blue garden is to be beautiful as well as to be blue.

— GERTRUDE JEKYLL, garden designer, 1911

I get tired of safe plantings of pale blue, silver, and white. Though people bristle at orange, gold, or scarlet, they all have a place, and a good place, in our gardens. No color is impossible to work with, and sometimes the most unlikely ones—like orange, or magenta— make the most exciting effects.

━ MARCO STUFANO, director of Horticulture, Wave Hill, New York, quoted in The *American Mixed Border* by Ann Lovejoy, 1993

Anyone who devoted his entire life to blue flowers, even if he limited himself to the most beautiful of them all, the delphinium, would find himself at the end of a 90-year life still confronted with a blue infinity of work still to be done. . . .

━ KARL FOERSTER, *The New Delphinium: Story of a Passion*, 1929

Yellow is a controversial colour. People shy away from mauve as a word but are perfectly content to grow the majority of mauve flowers provided they are discreetly described as lavender or lilac. With yellow it is the color itself that frightens them. There are many keen gardeners who have to let you know, as soon as gardens, and plants start to be discussed, that they are not prepared to tolerate yellow or orange flowers.

━ CHRISTOPHER LLOYD, *The Well Tempered Garden*, 1985

The Grape Hyacinth is the favorite spring flower of my garden— but no! I thought a minute ago the Scilla was! And what place has the Violet? The Flower de Luce? I cannot decide, but this I know— it is some blue flower.

━ ALICE MORSE EARLE, *The Blue Flower Border, Old-Time Gardens*, 1901

We are constantly trying to bring the sky down to our gardens.

━ RICHARDSON WRIGHT, *Another Gardener's Bed-Book*, 1933, on the passion for blue flowers

Colour seemed flung down anyhow, anywhere; every sort of colour, piled up in heaps, pouring along in rivers.

━ ELIZABETH VON ARNIM, *Enchanted April*, 1922

For years I have avoided magenta with feverish zest. I do not like it. It kills my henna reds. It fights with the cedar brown of my cottage. Yet every year something of that hue intrudes. If it isn't sweet william reverting to type, it is a red phlox gone decadent.

— MARGARET GOLDSMITH, "The Perils of Gardening," *Scribners* magazine, June 1936

In the end, color combinations come down to our personal preferences, which we must discover through observation and experiment.

— MONTAGU DON, *The Sensuous Garden*, 1997

Magenta is so universally despised and shunned. Not only is it deprived of its proper foils, but it is nearly always set down beside those colours surest to bring out its worst side. I am very fond of this colour as worn by flowers and have taken some trouble to bring it into harmony with its surroundings.

I do not deny that there are poor and wishy-washy tones of magenta and that these are not desirable, but where the colour is frank and pure and used with a right intermingling of green and other soft friendly hues, there is none more beautiful and distinctive.

— LOUISE BEEBE WILDER, *Colour in My Garden*, 1918

Gardeners take brown for granted. It is there unnoticed, unconsidered as a color. Yet after green it is by far the predominant hue in our vision at any one time, and from mid-winter through to late spring it even overwhelms green, with brown bark, twigs, and above all, brown soil.

— MONTAGU DON, *The Sensuous Garden*, 1997

I'm not at all convinced that magenta is dreadful. It doesn't look especially good near the hot orange of marigolds, butterfly weed, or tiger lilies, but then little else does.

— ALLEN LACY, *The Gardener's Eye and other essays*, 1992

Orange and pink make uncomfortable flower-bedfellows. Orange makes pink saccharine and coy, and pink brings the slut out of orange.

    — MONTAGU DON, *The Sensuous Garden*, 1997

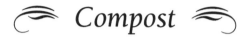 *Compost*

People who love compost can drive you crazy, eyeing your eggshell well before you've finished your egg.

    — DIANA WELLS, "Manure, Sweet Manure," *Green Prints*, Spring 1998

It took years to learn what would not grow here. I like to say I have the greatest catalogue of plants in my compost heap.

    — HAROLD EPSTEIN, rock gardener, quoted in "The Everest of Rock Gardens," by Linda Yang, *The New York Times*, November 21, 1991

Gardeners, like infants, are proud of their waste products.

    — HUGH POPHAM, *Gentleman Peasants: A Gardener's ABC*, 1968

In American gardening the successful compost pile seems to have supplanted the perfect hybrid tea rose or the gigantic beefsteak tomato as the outward signs of horticultural grace.

    — MICHAEL POLLAN, "Cultivating Virtue," *Harpers* magazine, May 1987

Behold this compost! behold it well!
What chemistry!
Earth grows such sweet things out of such corruptions.

    — WALT WHITMAN, "This Compost," 1867

Decayed literature makes the best soil.
  ━ THOREAU (1817–1862)

Container/Indoor Gardening

Plants in pots are like animals in a zoo—they're totally dependent on their keepers.
  ━ JOHN VAN DE WATER, "Potted Plants," *Star-Ledger*, 1996

Roof gardening is one of life's great pleasures, and is not referred to as container gardening for nothing. Everything is manageable, deadheading is a doddle, weeding non-existent, and you can re-organise colour schemes by shifting the pots around. The disadvantages are removing the debris, heaving bags of peat up several flights, ceaseless watering and, if you are very unlucky and misjudge the weight, house subsidence.
  ━ CLARE HASTINGS, from *Gardening Letters to My Daughter* by Anne Scott James, 1991

The last Friday in July is "Take Your Houseplants for a Walk Day."
  ━ *The Herb Companion*, Oct/Nov 1988

For the most part, I raise only the commonest, easiest plants and flowering bulbs. Once in a while I take a flyer and try a difficult exotic. Orchids I abjure entirely, for lack of time. But even with this modest program, I become, in winter, a sort of floor nurse in my spare moments—taking temperatures, rubbing backs, and making a thousand small adjustments when my patients summon me.
  ━ KATHERINE S. WHITE, *Onward and Upward in the Garden*, 1958

Remember that your plants don't need you as much as you may think they do.

— FRANCES TENENBAUM, *Taylor's Guide to Houseplants*, 1987

And these [house]plants are much like the Vietnam War—once you have invested enough labor and woe, you are strangely unwilling to acknowledge that it was a stupid mistake to begin with. You just go on and on.

— HENRY MITCHELL, garden writer (1923–1993)

I love a railing even better than a plant table, because the railing is usually higher, bringing small plants closer to eye level, elevating them to major garden importance. With a line of container plants upon it, a railing becomes the Orient Express of gardening adventures, a train of enchantments.

— GEORGE SCHENK, *Gardening with Friends*, 1992

A nursery plant comes from parent stock in the same way as the slip or division I've acquired from a friend or neighbor, with only this difference: it has spent its life in a plastic pot, moving here and there on a truck bed, living on Peters and Pro-gro. I pity and want to console nursery plants for their hothouse tenderness, their lack of heritage, their lack of *ground*.

— MICHAEL FOX, "Grandmother and Her Peonies," from *My Favorite Plant* by Jamaica Kincaid, 1998

Keep in mind that the average home is 5 percent drier than the Sahara Desert, has almost no air movement and usually poor light. These are hardly ideal conditions for plants.

— PHIL TACKTILL, of the Jiu San Bonsai Company, on the challenges of growing bonsai indoors, *The New York Times*, December 29, 1990

Plant losses in container gardening bother me much less than they once did. Nowadays I'm content with the sure knowledge that I'm composing plants for the short term.

— GEORGE SCHENK, *Gardening with Friends*, 1992

Stop bothering with houseplants unless you have absolutely no earth of your own outside. Two houseplants in one house are plenty—you will need all the windowsills for cuttings and trays of seeds.
　— JOSEPHINE SAXTON, *Gardening Down a Rabbit Hole*, 1996

Control

In the last analysis there is only one common factor between all gardens, and that is control of nature by man. Control, that is, for aesthetic reasons.
　— HUGH JOHNSON, *The Principles of Gardening*, 1996

I had committed the original sin of gardening, thinking I could impose my own will on my garden, thinking I could compel roses to grow in the shadows of oak trees, believe me, you might more usefully invest your time in making water run uphill.
　— OTTO FRIEDRICH, "Of Apple Trees and Roses," *TIME* magazine, June 20, 1988

The mastery of nature is vainly believed to be an adequate substitute for self-mastery.
　— REINHOLD NIEBUHR, American theologian (1892–1971)

No garden is ever subdued. On the day your hand falls powerless by your side it multiplies efforts to run wild.
　— S. L. BENSUSAN, "Trowel Work," *The New York Times Magazine*, May 15, 1949

The garden shudders when it hears the back door slam and recognizes my footsteps upon the back porch. By now it knows the man it is dealing with: a harsh but just master who brooks no nonsense from flora or weed.

➤ RUSSELL BAKER, American humorist (1925–)

The "control of nature" is a phrase conceived in arrogance, born of the Neandrathal age of biology and philosophy when it was supposed that nature exists for the convenience of man.

➤ RACHEL CARSON, *Silent Spring*, 1962

Man masters nature not by force but by understanding. This is why science has succeeded where magic failed: because it has looked for no spell to cast on nature.

➤ JACOB BRONOWSKI, *Universities Quarterly*, 1956, quoted in *The Gardener's Bug Book*, 1994

Cottage Gardening

My general advice to would-be cottage gardeners is to start small, be prepared for the expense (these borders seem to eat plants for lunch), and be sure that you are ready to spend a lot of time in the garden!

➤ MICHAEL WEISHAN, *The New Traditional Garden*, 1999

For most of us who are intimidated by theories of garden design, the cottage garden provides immediate appeal, since it is a horticultural rather than an architectural solution to a limited area.

➤ PATRICIA THORPE, "Stop Mowing, Start Digging," *The New York Times*, October 14, 1990

There is a great deal of freedom in cottage gardening, which may be the primary reason it is so appealing. There is an element of chance. As plants are allowed to self sow they seem to move about on their own (though usually under the gently guiding hand of the gardener), and the look of the garden changes subtly from year to year.

— RUTH ROHDE HASKELL, "American Cottage Gardens," *Brooklyn Botanic Garden Record*, 1990

Unruly plants growing in tangled informality. Sweet fragrances, soft colours, the hum of bees and the flutter of butterflies. Perhaps the gentle whisper of leaves or the murmur of water. Add these to a neat white cottage with a thatched roof where apple blossom never fades and the sun always shines and we have cottage garden.

— PHILIP SWINDELLS, *Cottage Gardening in Town and Country*, 1986

A haphazard mix of plants is usually a hodge-podge, and that's not a cottage garden—that's a mess.

— RUTH ROHDE HASKELL, "American Cottage Gardens," *Brooklyn Botanic Garden Record*, 1990

Cottage gardens are the most wonderful excuses for combining everything from peonies and chives to apple trees and roses.

— MARGARET HENSEL, *English Cottage Gardening for American Gardeners*, 1992

Every blossoming square in cottage gardens seen from flying windows of the train has its true and touching message for the traveller, and stirs delightful thought.

— MRS. FRANCIS KING, *The Well-Considered Garden*, 1915

⤚ *Cut Flowers* ⤙

The reds, pinks, and magentas I mix fearlessly and, if I possessed one, I should put them in a chalice of brilliant hard green malachite. There are qualities in the red of geraniums, and in the green of malachite, which have something to say to each other; together they make a note of shouting triumph quite indescribable, and quite outside one's usual ideas of colour combination.
  ⤚ CONSTANCE SPRY, *A Constance Spry Anthology*, 1953

The excitement and passion which flowers could arouse then was of a wholly different order to any floral emotion which exists today. If, in the twentieth century, a vase of cultivated flowers is appealing, pretty, and, for all but the keen enthusiast, slightly banal, for a Dutch person of the Golden Age it could be an object with an allure of heady luxury and faintly delicious wickedness.
  ⤚ PAUL TAYLOR, *Dutch Flower Painting*, 1995

The joy of being able to cut flowers freely . . . is an end that justifies a lot of gardening effort.
  ⤚ T. H. EVERETT, English horticulturist and author (1903–1986)

What more delightsome than an infinite variete of sweet smelling flowers? Decking with sundry colours the greene mantle of the Earth, the universall Mother of us all, so by them bespotted, so dyed, that all the world cannot sample them, and wherein it is more fit to admire the Dyer, than imitate his workemanship. Colouring not onely the earth, but decking the ayre, and sweetning every breath and spirit.
  ⤚ WILLIAM LAWSON, *A New Orchard and Garden*, 1618

The flower arranger who is not a gardener should never be let loose with a knife or scissors out of doors.
  ⤚ BOLAND SISTERS, old wive's lore

Arranging flowers is like writing in that it is an art of choice. Not everything can be used of the rich material that rushes forward demanding utterance. And just as one tries one word after another, puts a phrase together only to tear it apart, so one arranges flowers. It is engrossing work, and needs a fresh eye and a steady hand. When you think the thing is finished, it may suddenly topple over, or look too crowded after all, or a little meager. It needs one more note of bright pink, or it needs white. . . . After that first hour I have used up my "seeing energy" for a while, just as, after three hours at my desk, the edge begins to go, the critical edge.

— MAY SARTON, *Plant Dreaming Deep*, 1968

Design

I believe that visiting historic gardens and looking at the old formal ways of gardening is an essential prelude to making your own garden. . . .There does exist a "grammar" of design and if you learn this first, from looking and reading, you can adapt the principles to a geometric layout or to freer more naturalistic concepts.

— PENELOPE HOBHOUSE, *A Gardener's Journal*, 1997

You have to have an idea. If you don't have a concept, you're just making goulash.

— WILLIAM BRINCKA, sculptor-gardener, Indiana, quoted in "By the Sculptor's Hand," by Carolyn Ulrich, *Horticulture*, May 1990

Restraint is a fundamental principle of good gardening. Simplicity brings a sense of calm, whereas too many ideas and too much variety creates a sense of restlessness.

— PENELOPE HOBHOUSE, *A Gardener's Journal*, 1997

Through all the variations due to climate, country, history and the natural idiosyncrasy of man which have appeared in the evolution of the garden through successive civilisations, certain principles remain constant however much their application may change. Perhaps the greatest of these, and the one most lacking in the average garden today, is a sense of unity. It is a quality found in all great landscapes, based on the rhythm of natural land-form, the domination of one type of vegetation and the fact that human use and buildings have kept in sympathy with their surroundings. When we say that a landscape has been spoilt we mean that it has lost this unity.

— DAME SYLVIA CROWE, garden designer, 1951

You have to think and think to get something simple.

— RON LUTSKO, garden designer, quoted in *Breaking Ground: Portraits of Ten Garden Designers* by Page Dickey, 1997

Whether the approach is a footpath or a road, it should be direct and without horticultural distractions. The entrance is a focus or magnet drawing you toward it, and any complicated landscaping will disturb.

— RUSSELL PAGE, *The Education of a Gardener*, 1962

Too often gardeners focus solely on flower color, allowing the greens to occur haphazardly, but green is the color that pulls everything together and deserves to be planned.

— JEFF COX, *Creating a Garden for the Senses*, 1993

The very meanest Gardeners, who, laying aside the Rake and Spade, take upon them to give Designs of Gardens, when they understand nothing of the Matter. Unhappy are those that fall into the Hands of such Persons, who put them to a great Expence to plant a sorry Garden, when it costs no more to execute a good Design, than an ill one! The same Trees and Plants are constantly made use of, and produce an ill Effect through their Bad Disposition.

— A. J. DEZALLIER A'ARGENVILLE, *The Theory and Practice of Gardening*, 1712

All art must grow out of native soil.
— JENS JENSEN, landscape designer (1860–1950)

Atmosphere is the most important element in a garden. A lawn with low bright borders next to a wire fence does not have atmosphere, or to be exact, it does; sad and bleak.
— JOSEPHINE SAXTON, *Gardening Down a Rabbit Hole*, 1996

When people ask me for an English border, I think what they really mean is overblown.
— NANCY GOSLEE POWERS, garden designer, quoted in *Breaking Ground: Portraits of Ten Garden Designers* by Page Dickey, 1997

I know one successful front garden with a central path to the front door where the rectangular panels on either side are simple box hedges enclosing mown grass.
— PENELOPE HOBHOUSE, *The Smaller Garden*, 1981

A couple of brick steps not set at the right angle to the paths leading to them or a path of bricks to a garden tank that has not been set in line with the house wall near, are fearful eyesores. A garden planned on formal lines needs to be very accurate and correct.
— A. M. MARTINEAU, 1923

Compared to designers in other fields, gardeners have a trickier time succeeding on a visual level, since our building blocks are alive, with schedules and needs that might not fit a particular decorating scheme.
— ADAM LEVINE, "Zone Envy," *Garden Design*, April 1999

"Mr. Brown, I very earnestly desire that I may die before you."
"Why so?"
"Because I should like to see heaven before you have improved it."
— Anonymous anecdote told of Capability Brown, eighteenth-century landscape designer

Gardening, like all field of design, is subject to the whims of personal taste, the vagaries of fashion, the biases of region and social class, and the shifting tides of pop culture.

➤ DOUGLAS BRENNER, "What Modern Means," *Garden Design*, February/March 1999

Vita refuses to abide by our decision or to remove the miserable little trees which stand in the way of my design. The romantic temperament as usual obstructing the classic.

➤ HAROLD NICOLSON, English author (1886–1968)

Obviously a garden is not the wilderness but an assembly of shapes, most of them living, that owes some share of its composition, its appearance, to human design and effort, human conventions and convenience, and the human pursuit of that elusive, indefinable harmony that we call beauty. It has a life of its own, an intricate, willful, secret life, as any gardener knows. It is only the humans in it who think of it as a garden. But a garden is a relation, which is one of the countless reasons why it is never finished.

➤ W. S. MERWIN, "It's a Jungle out There," *House and Garden*, March 1997

The weakness of American gardening is the petunia-bed thinking of many who play a leading role in it, and a lack of understanding of it as environment.

➤ CARLTON B. LEES, *Gardens, Plants and Man*, 1970

Digging

The lovable part of planting is digging the little holes in the ground and the difficult part is finding a clean bit of arm to rub your forehead with where the midges, bats, etc., have been biting it.

➤ W. C. SELLAR and R. J. Y EASTMAN, *Garden Rubbish & Other Country Bumps*, 1937

Digging, done well, is a kind of practical dance. The choreography of the spade is fluid, economical, circular. It bears intention forward into action and round to intention again. The best digging often appears effortless. There is no waste, no rushing, no haphazard fits and starts, only the deliberate downward sweep of the blade, an easy arcing upswing, and steadily accumulating evidence of progress. Digging may never qualify as a spectator sport, but good digging is surprisingly fun to watch, and good diggers, as a rule, are not nearly so irritable while under observation as their less-accomplished peers.

— J. TEVERE MACFADYEN, "The Call to Dig," *Horticulture*, March 1985

Everyone who has done much digging knows the effect it has not only on the mind and body but on one's whole being . . . for solid ever changing unfailing enjoyment give me digging.

— ELEANOUR ROHDE, *A Garden of Herbs*, 1920

Some people are like ants. Give them a warm day and a piece of ground and they start digging. There the similarity ends. Ants keep on digging. Most people don't. They establish contact with the soil, absorb so much vernal vigor that they can't stay in one place, and desert the fork or spade to see how the rhubarb is coming and whether the asparagus is yet in sight.

— HAL BORLAND, *The New York Times*, April 27, 1947

A lady, with a small light spade may, by repeatedly digging over the same line, and taking out only a little earth at a time, succeed in doing all the digging that can be required in a small garden; and she will not only have the satisfaction of seeing the garden created as it were, by her own hands, but she will find her health and spirits wonderfully improved by the exercise, and by the reviving smell of the fresh earth.

— JANE LOUDON, *Gardening for Ladies*, 1840

 *Dirt*

The love of dirt is among the earliest of passions as it is the latest. Mudpies gratify one of our first and best instincts. So long as we are dirty we are pure. Fondness for the ground comes back to a man after he has run the round of pleasure and business, eaten dirt, and sown wild oats, drifted about the world, and taken the wind of all its moods. The love of digging in the ground, is as sure to come back to him, as he is sure, at last, to go under the ground, and stay there.

— CHARLES DUDLEY WARNER, *My Summer in a Garden*, 1870

In the spring, at the end of the day, you should smell like dirt.

— MARGARET ATWOOD, Canadian novelist (1939–)

I am open to the accusation that I see compost as an end in itself. But we do grow some real red damn tomatoes such as you can't get in the stores. And potatoes, beans, lettuce, collards, onions, squash, cauliflower, eggplant, carrots, peppers. *Dirt* in your own backyard, producing things you eat. Makes you wonder.

— ROY BLOUNT, JR., American writer (1941–)

The real lowdown on gardening is . . . dirt.

— TEXAS BIX BENDER, author (1949–)

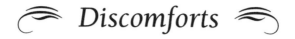 Discomforts

Caterpillars crawl on me and rosebugs creep down my neck. I kneel where the dogs have preceded me. I lug stones around and they fall on my toes, making funny black spots. My knees ache, and I am tanned in strange places.

— ANONYMOUS, Contributor's Club, "Watching Things Grow," *The Atlantic Monthly*, July 1936

What knee pads really do is to save your back. Most people hate to get down on their knees because it's uncomfortable and often the ground is wet or muddy. So they end up bending over the whole time their weeding or whatever, and pretty soon they've got back problems.

— PHIL COLSON, garden center manager, *The Expert's Book of Garden Hints*, 1993

The hardest thing to raise in my garden is my knees.

— ANONYMOUS

It must be admitted that one of the great drawbacks to gardening and weeding is the state into which the hands and fingers get. Unfortunately, one's hands belong not only to oneself, but to the family, who do not scruple to tell the gardening amateur that her appearance is "revolting."

— MRS. C. W. EARLE, *Pot-Pourri from a Surrey Garden*, 1897

I haven't felt so worked out in years. Every visit to the garden is the same. I'm just wiped out in a wonderful way.

— TWINKA THIEBAUD, caterer, Los Angeles, who abandoned a health club for gardening, quoted in "Paradise Found," *TIME* magazine, June 20, 1988

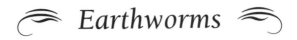 *Earthworms*

The gardener with soil full of earth worms can bless himself, for they are a sign of good tilth and fertility. But they don't go willingly about their useful work in poor, hard ground where they are most needed. It's another case of them as has, gets.

— ELEANOR PERÉNYI, *Green Thoughts*, 1981

Intestines of the earth.

— ARISTOTLE, on earthworms

"I don't want to know about it. Don't show me where they are. And don't ask me to take care of them if you go out of town!"

— Joan Durrant Fulsinger's daughter upon hearing that her mother was taking up worm composting, *Fine Gardening*, August 1997

One favorable aspect of having worms as pets is that you can go away without having to make arrangements with the vet. . . . It really is amazing to reach into my worm bin and pull out a handful of rich sweet soil, wriggling with worms.

— ANNE RAVER, *The New York Times*, January 23, 1994

The earthworm is almost alone among invertebrates in the tenderness he inspires.

— WILLIAM BRYANT LOGAN, *Dirt: The Ecstatic Skin of the Earth*, 1995

It has been a complete surprise to me how many persons have cared for the subject.

— CHARLES DARWIN, on his last book, *The Formation of Vegetable Mould Through the Actions of Worms, With Observations on Their Habits*, 1881, which became a bestseller, outperforming all of his published work, including *Origin of Species*

⌇ *English Gardens* ⌇

Our England is a garden that is full of stately views, Of borders, beds and shrubberies and lawns and avenues, with statues on the terraces and peacocks strutting by, but the glory of the Garden lies in more than meets the eye.

— RUDYARD KIPLING, "The Glory of the Garden," *Sixty Poems,* 1939

The French painter Claude Lorraine remarked that there are only two branches of the fine arts—painting and pastry-cooking. That may be the case for the French. For the English, I like to think that there are two fine arts too—painting and the creation of gardens. Of the two, I would say that we are lucky enough, through climate and inclination, to excel at the second.

— ANDREW LAWSON, "The Art of Gardens," *Hortus,* Summer 1990

I found myself growing uneasy with a notion that America held much unsuspected sweetness . . . and then the delegates of the Garden Club of America came over to see our English gardens, and that was the finishing touch. For their enthusiasm was most infectious. Their flower knowledge was a great delight to those of us who had hardly realized that there *were* any gardens in America.

— MARION CRAN, *How Does Your Garden Grow?,* 1935

What gardens meant to their owners has differed in every century and they reveal as much about the character and preoccupations of the men and women who made them as any other art form. That is the real glory of the English Garden.

— MARY KEEN, *The Glory of the English Garden,* 1990

English landscape was invented by gardeners imitating foreign painters who were evoking classical authors. The whole thing was brought home in the luggage from the grand tour.

— TOM STOPPARD, "Arcadia," 1993

I don't like him. He's an Englishman, and I expect he's fond of dwarf conifers.

— Tom Hay, Scottish gardener, quoted in "Capitalizing on Conifers" by Christopher Reed, *Horticulture*, October 1985

And make us as Newton was, who in his garden watching
The apple falling towards England, became aware
Between himself and her of an eternal tie.

— Wystan Hugh Auden, *Orators*, 1932, dedication

So favourable to vegetation is the climate of this happy island, that we can, with care, raise every shrub, plant, and tree,that flourishes in any part of the world. In fact, we can make the World of Vegetation our own!

— Gilbert Brookes, *The Complete British Gardener*, 1779

Garden design remains one corner of the culture in which our dependence on Britain has never been broken.

— Michael Pollan, "Cultivating Virtue," *Harpers* magazine, May 1987, on American gardens

If life becomes a little dull, look into any English gardening book and see how many plant pests and diseases are called American.

— Richardson Wright, *Another Gardener's Bed-Book*, 1933

Indeed it seems to me no small reproach to the English Nation, that we suffer so many French Books of Gardening to be obtruded upon us, containing Rules calculated for another Climate and which tend to lead us into many Errors!

— John Laurence, *The Fruit-Garden Kalendar*, 1718

There is much more than meets the eye in English Gardens. Even the most insignificant have their story to tell, for every stage of English history is reflected in them. They have gradually changed through the centuries, and each phase of our political development, our foreign policy, our wars, and our discoveries has left its mark on our gardens.

— Alicia Amherst, *Historic Gardens of England*, 1938

Environmental Issues

Hurt not the earth, neither the sea nor the trees.
— *The Bible*, Revelations 7:3

Our attitude toward plants is a singularly narrow one. If we see any immediate utility in a plant we foster it. If for any reason we find the presence undesirable or merely a matter of indifference, we may condemn it to destruction forthwith.
— RACHEL CARSON, *Silent Spring*, 1962

Next to having a nuclear power plant in your front yard, having a lawn is about as environmentally incorrect as you can get these days.
— ABBY ADAMS, *The Gardener's Gripe Book*, 1995

I haven't nuked this piece of earth with herbicides, as many books advise. I have simply dug out the weeds that were there and let the ground rest for a couple of weeks. I know there will be plenty of weeds, but hey, this is a wild garden.
— ANNE RAVER, *Deep in the Green*, 1995

From an ecological viewpoint, gardening is the essence of disturbance, a ramshackle pseudoecosystem that has evolved piecemeal from seeds and tubers in our prehistoric ancestor's garbage piles. Most garden plants not only thrive on but require constant disturbance. Of course, we call that disturbance by names like "care" and "cultivation," because its results care and cultivate us, but anybody who has ever dug into the dirt and turned up a clod full of hysterical earthworms knows what he is doing to their little world.
— DAVID RAINS WALLACE, *The Untamed Garden and Other Personal Essays*, 1986

Ladybugs work hard for us in the garden, and there's no charge. Whoever taught youngsters to chant "ladybug, ladybug fly away home" was definitely not a gardener.

— RUTH PAGE, *Ruth Page's Gardening Journal*, 1989

It is unthinkable for gardeners to knowingly add to the destruction of these little patriarchs [wild bulbs], the floral gene sources of the planet. You can, quite simply, screen out all wild bulbs offered and become an effective defense attorney at once for the little wild, patriarch bulbs without whose genes there would be no tulips, no daffodils and no catalogues. No one will want to be caught wielding a "smoking trowel" . . . DO NOT WIELD THE SMOKING TROWEL!!!

— MARJORIE ARUNDEL, *Bulletin of the Garden Club of America*, August 1989

Its discovery is a shining example of the way in which scientific effort applied correctly can benefit mankind.

— W. F. BEWLEY, *Science Has Green Fingers: An Authoritative Guide to the Science of Good Gardening*, 1959, on DDT

After several years of DDT spray, the town is almost devoid of robins and starlings; chickadees have not been on my [feeder] shelf for two years, and this year the cardinals are gone too . . .

It is hard to explain to the children that the birds have been killed off, when they have learned in school that a Federal law protects the birds from killing or capture. "Will they ever come back?" they ask, and I do not have the answer. The elms are still dying, and so are the birds. *Is* anything being done? *Can* anything be done? Can *I* do anything?

— HOUSEWIFE FROM HINSDALE, Illinois, in a letter to the prominent ornithologist, Robert Cushman Murphy, curator emeritus of Birds at the American Museum of Natural History, quoted in *Silent Spring* by Rachel Carson, 1962

Mentioning fungi to gardeners usually conjures up alarmist visions of rusts and wilts, if not the dreaded honey fungus, but there's another side to the picture. The seasonal appearance of fungus fruit on your lawn can be a cause for celebration—both for their intrinsic beauty and fascination, and for their value in indicating vestiges of a vanishing pollution-free world.

— PENNY DAVID, "Gems of Nature," *Gardens Illustrated*, October 1999

We had better find a way to grow things in asphalt before we cover the world with it.

— ROGER B. SWAIN, *Groundwork: A Gardener's Ecology*, 1994

[Rodale's] bearded countenance glared forth from the editorial page like that of an Old Testament prophet in those days (since his death it has been supplanted by the more benign one of his son), and his message was stamped on every page. Like all great messages, it was simple, and to those of us hearing it for the first time, a blinding revelation. Soil, he told us, isn't a substance to hold up plants in order that they may be fed with artificial fertilizers, and we who treated it as such were violating the cycle of nature. We must give back what we took away.

— ELEANOR PERÉNYI, *Green Thoughts*, 1981, on J. I. Rodale, founding editor of *Organic Gardening*

If the history of the soil were taught to us in grade school, most of us would know at a young age what can happen when the people of any society stop paying close attention to the relationship between the health of their soil and their own sustenance.

— JIM NOLLMAN, *Why We Garden*, 1994

Insects do a great job of controlling themselves if we don't foul up the balance by spraying pesticides.

— J. HOWARD GARRETT, *The Dirt Doctor's Guide to Organic Gardening*, 1995

Although Bt is natural in that it has a biological origin, it's questionable whether spraying is a natural use of it. It is not an infectious organism, not a caterpillar disease. It is a soil organism, a decayer, that has no known relationship with insects. . . .

One must ask, is the meeting of a soil spore with a gypsy moth caterpillar on an oak leaf natural? And is the death itself—a case of mistaken identity, a protein fragment grasped in good faith because it is similar to one that gut cells ordinarily welcome—a natural event?

— SARA STEIN, *Noah's Garden,* 1993

America's landscapes are lawn-dominated, and lawns occupy an area equal to the size of the state of Michigan. In addition to offering little or nothing of value to wildlife, lawns are the largest consumer of landscape water, of pesticides, and of fertilizers in our urbanizing areas. Mower noise and fumes pollute our neighborhoods. Grass clippings add significantly to our landfills. Gradually get rid of fifty percent or more of your lawn. Trees, shrub masses, ground covers, flower beds, prairie or meadow patches, and attractively mulched areas are much better environmental choices, for people and for wildlife.

— The National Wildlife Federation, 1990

They make a Walden Pond out of their home, their grounds, and their activities. It is the purpose of our compost and our avoidance of poisons to preserve the web of life in our garden.

— ROBERT RODALE, **on organic gardeners,** 1970s

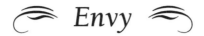 *Envy*

. . . at a dog-trot on the way to the train one morning we pass Neighbor Foster's house and see his side yard all spaded and raked and the brown earth smells just wonderful. (Foster's an aggravating type; he's always the first one to have his storm windows off and his screens on, and he paints his rose trellis every year.)

— C. B. PALMER, "Memoir Written with a Non-Green Thumb," *The New York Times Magazine*, June 12, 1949

In a nutshell, I was sorry because I had no *lorapetalum*, and then I met a man who had no snowdrop.

— HENRY MITCHELL, "The Wrongs of Winter, The Rites of Spring," *Green Prints*, Winter 1990–1991

Certainly, but against all expectation, a garden, if it does not exactly become a battlefield, is often not the least likely place in the world for a display of envy and uncharitableness.

— GEOFFREY TAYLOR, *The Gardeners's Album*, 1954

There is nothing in the whole realm of gardening which arouses so much pride and adoration or, if it belongs to your neighbour, so much envy and all uncharitableness, as a really vast stack of crusty, well-matured, asphyxiating, Vintage *Ding*.

— W. C. SELLAR and R. J. Y EASTMAN, *Garden Rubbish & Other Country Bumps*, 1937

There is no garden in England or France I envy, and not one I'd swap for mine: this is the aim of gardening—not to make us complacent idiots, exactly, but to make us content and calm for a time. . . . It's all right for fancy people to head for lush places, but a gardener should stay steady and stay home.

— HENRY MITCHELL, *One Man's Garden*, 1992

I rarely envy a man the possession of his wife, or his maidservant or his cattle . . . but there are times when I maul the tenth commandment without a qualm. That is when he has a *Meconopsis* I cannot grow, an *Eremerus* that I have sworn to own, or a *Silene Hookeri* that defies my horticultural blandishments. In the presence of these I not only jettison the tenth, but also have misgivings about the sixth commandment.

⤙ RICHARDSON WRIGHT, *Another Gardener's Bed-Book*, 1933

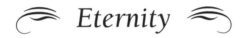 *Eternity*

About two miles from Farnham is More-park, formerly the seat of Sir William Temple, who, by his will, ordered his heart to be put into a china basin, and buried under a sun-dial in his garden, which was accordingly performed.

⤙ DANIEL DEFOE, *A Tour Through the Island of Great Britain*, 1724

We do not feel, as Humphrey Repton, the landscape gardener, felt in his epitaph, that our dust is going to turn into roses. Dust we believe simply to be dust.

⤙ GEOFFREY GRIGSON, writer (1905–1985)

Close beside a fir tree three sheep are grazing. Stand by the tree and think yourself into it. . . . Stretch up your spirit towards its topmost branches following each changing urge of growth. Sense its growth, for growth is immortality. We are all but cells, forming and reforming in the elemental tissue, momentary manifestations, glimpses in the microscopes of God. What does the chlorophyll cell in the blade of grass know of biology? Just as much perhaps as we do of eternity.

⤙ ROBERT GIBBINGS, poet, quoted in *Trees: A Celebration*, 1990

Trees are the best monuments that a man can erect to his own memory. They speak his praises without flattery, and they are blessings to children yet unborn.

➤ LORD ORRERY to Thomas Carew, 1749

I can only hope that, if I ever get past the Pearly Gates, I shan't be made a member of the orchestra and put to twanging a harp, but will be assigned to the garden section, where I can wear my old corduroy pants and indescribably soiled work shirt and really have a chance to do all the many things I have left undone.

➤ RICHARDSON WRIGHT, *Another Gardener's Bed-Book*, 1933

Gardeners' Epitaph, 1662
Know, stranger, e'er thou pass, beneath this stone
Lie John Tradescant, grandsire, father, son . . .
These famous Antiquarians that had been
Both gardeners to the rose and Lily Queen
Transplanted now themselves, sleep here; and when
Angeles shall with their trumpets waken men
And fire shall purge the world, These hence shall rise
And change their gardens for a Paradise.

➤ Quoted in *A History of English Gardening* by G. W. Johnson, 1829

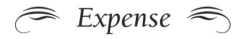

Expense

A garden has a curious innocent way of consuming cash while all the time you are under the illusion that you are spending nothing.

➤ ESTHER MEYNELL, *A Woman Talking*, 1940

I wish I could give you a cost estimate, but I haven't kept records, maybe intentionally.

➤ RANDALL FRIESEN, St. Charles, Missouri, passionate amateur award winner, *Garden Design* magazine December 1995/January 1996

Some people buy expensive tools just to show that they're a "member of the club," then the tools sit in the garage. None of them is better than the four posts and a bunch of chicken wire that my dad used to use.

➤ WILLIAM LOGAN, quoted in "The Latest Home Accessory: Garden Tools" by Eileen White Read, *The Wall Street Journal*, April 10, 1998

No one ever knows what one can't do, until one tries. That is the will o' the wisp hope that lures [the gardener] perpetually on into the slough of bills and reckless expenditure.

➤ REGINALD FARRER, plantsman (1880–1920)

What though his phlox and hollyhocks ere half a month demised?
What though his ampelopsis clambered not as advertised?
Though every seed was guaranteed and every standard true—
Forget, forgive they did not live! Believe, and buy anew!

➤ RUDYARD KIPLING (1865–1936)

. . . We will gladly send the management a jar of our wife's green-tomato pickle from last summer's crop—dark green, spicy, delicious, costlier than pearls when you figure the overhead.

➤ E. B. WHITE, American author (1899–1985)

In buying plants for the orchard or the garden, make it an inflexible rule never to buy a second-rate tree, shrub, vine, or seed of any kind, at any price, no matter how low, when you can get a first-rate article at a fair price. If you buy cheap goods of this kind because they are low-priced, you'll be sure to get what you bargain for. If you buy them below the real value of the best of their kind, you may be sure there is some "out" about them that you do not see.

➤ *The Old Farmer's Almanac*, 1881

When your garden is finished I hope it will be more beautiful than you anticipated, require less care than you expected, and have cost only a little more than you had planned.

➤ Last line of *Gardens Are for People* by THOMAS D. CHURCH, 1955

Fantasy Gardens

You don't have to garden to garden; gardening in the mind is a gentle vice with an impetus of its own.

➤ MIRABEL OSLER, *A Gentle Plea for Chaos: The Enchantment of Gardening*, 1989

The mood I seek above all is one of relaxation given by a garden easy and untortured, in which plants, however rare and strange, will grow and take their place naturally and discreetly.

➤ RUSSELL PAGE, *The Education of a Gardener*, 1962, describing a special garden he was planning for himself

If only one were as good a gardener in practice as one is in theory, what a garden one would create!

➤ VITA SACKVILLE-WEST, *Some Flowers*, 1937

Except that it would be a flagrant transgression of the right to privacy and the right to plant azaleas if you want to, I wouldn't mind seeing an ordinance enjoining the owners of new houses on naked lots to wait a year before they planted a single shrub or tree after they get the lawn in, requiring them to visit specialty nurseries, study nursery catalogues, and go to a good arboretum once a month. . . . While I'm imagining this oppressive piece of legislation, I might as well set up a new political office, the Commissar of Plant Diversity. It would be this person's job to see to it that every front yard in a given neighborhood had one tree and one shrub in it that none of the neighbors was growing. . . . The effect would be to make a neighborhood itself an arboretum.

— ALLEN LACY, *The Garden in Autumn*, 1990

It has always been my aim to have as large a garden as possible, to be tended with the least work, and to provide interest and beauty of flower and foliage throughout the year.

— GRAHAM STUART THOMAS, *Three Gardens of Pleasant Flowers*, 1983

Sometimes my garden seems like a mirage always receding but if ever this intermittent vision becomes a reality, wherever it is, whatever its size and shape it will be satisfying for like all gardens it will be a world for itself and for me.

— RUSSELL PAGE, *The Education of a Gardener*, 1962

I enjoy our garden in my mind. I have been in it, thought about it, planned it so often and so long that I know it like the proverbial back of my hand.

— MICHAEL DOWER, "Living with the Garden," *The Countryman*, Summer 1974

Imaginary gardens, forever sunlit, free of bugs and blights, grow in the mind and gleam like Oz, promise a vernal afterlife, illuminate January.

— BARBARA HOLLAND, *Endangered Pleasures*, 1995

I sleep deeply, twigs and leaves in my hair, dreaming of the crocuses and daffodils that will bloom from my efforts.

➤ MARGARET PIERPONT, "Becoming Itself," *Green Prints*, Spring 1993

Half the interest of a garden is the constant exercise of the imagination. I believe that people entirely devoid of imagination never can be really good gardeners.

➤ MRS. C. W. EARLE, *Pot-Pourri from a Surrey Garden*, 1897

January gardens may be the best gardens of all. One thing for sure, I've never seen one make it intact to July.

➤ PAT STONE, "View from the Garden," *National Gardening* magazine, January/February 1994

Favorite/Least Favorite Plants

I do not want to go through life without *Polygonum aubertii*, with racemes of white, lightly perfumed flowers blooming almost all summer, although I know well how troublesome it is to keep in bounds. Ideally I would grow it up a dying forest tree and let it reach for the stars.

➤ HENRY MITCHELL, "A Garden in the City," The Essential Earthman, 1988

It has no redeeming social, economic, or horticultural value. It elicits frustration, tears, depression, rage, and ultimately, the urge to kill. Yet its survivability rivals that of the cockroach. This utterly worthless organism, this affront to all decent, hard-working tillers of the soil, is called witchgrass.

➤ JACK COOK, "Wiping Out Witchgrass," *Horticulture*, April 1989

Can words describe the fragrance of the very breath of spring—that delicious commingling of the perfume of arbutus, the odor of pines, and now-soaked soil just warming into life? Those who know the flower only as it is sold in the city streets, tied with wet dirty string into tight bunches, withered and forlorn can have little idea of the joy of finding the pink, pearly blossoms freshly opened among the withered leaves of oak and chestnut, moss, and pine needles in which they nestle close to the cold earth in the leafless, windy northern forest.

— NELTJE BLANCHAU, *Nature's Garden*, 1900

Notwithstanding one's determination to rise manfully above prejudice of all kinds, one may not always succeed 100 percent. I won't say that when I read in a seed catalog "a useful bedding plant for extra dry areas—gas stations, traffic islands, etc.," I felt that I had received any encouragement in my efforts to accept amaranthus as a respectable genus.

— ELISABETH SHELDON, *The Flamboyant Garden*, 1997

There are some flowers about which there is nothing interesting to say, except that they happen to have caught one's fancy. Such a flower, so far as I am concerned, is Gerbera Jamesonii. It has no historical interest that I know of; no long record of danger and difficulty attending its discovery; no background of savage mountains and Asiatic climates. It carries, in fact, no romantic appeal at all. It has taken no man's life. It has to stand or fall on its own merits.

— VITA SACKVILLE-WEST, *Some Flowers*, 1937

Over the Sedums I will not linger, for I don't like them; over the delightful Sempervivums I dare not linger, for I like them so much.

— REGINALD FARRER, *My Rock-Garden*, 1908

Until a few months back I never paid sedums much mind. These unassuming little succulents—whose most common name is stonecrop and whose principal needs are a goodly amount of neglect, poor soil (one book on the genus gives a recipe for soil impoverishment), and drought—have never interested me. I like plants that demand a lot, show off once in a while, put out bloomwise and fumewise, even wilt dramatically on occasions. Sedums, for the most part, don't do any of these things.

➤ PATTI HAGEN, "Plant It, Ignore It and Enjoy," *The Wall Street Journal*, April 3, 1987.

A genus whose flowers are often of a greenish shade of yellow? You might think it would be less popular among keen plantsmen and gardeners, but this is not so. Euphorbias have a subtlety of colour and an elegance of form which has long recommended them to those with discriminating taste in such matters.

➤ ROGER TURNER, "Euphorbia Broteroi: A New Spurge from Spain and Portugal," *Hortus*, Spring 1995

People have to get over this geranium thing.

➤ KATHY PUFAHL, Beds & Borders, a wholesale nursery on Long Island, New York, on overused container plants

Like a gracious small-leaved weeping willow when it is not in flower, and a sheer waterfall of soft purple when it is.

➤ REGINALD FARRER, on buddleia, 1914

It is a flower to peer into. In order to appreciate its true beauty, you will have to learn to know it intimately. You must look closely at all its little squares and also turn its bell up towards you so that you can look right down into its depths, and see the queer semi-transparency of the strangely foreign, wine-coloured chalice. It is a sinister little flower, sinister in its mournful colours of decay.

➤ VITA SACKVILLE-WEST, on the meadow fritillary, *Some Flowers*, 1937

I don't have a salvia collection. I have a garden.

➤ BETSY CLEBSCH, whose northern California garden is populated with more than 100 species and cultivars of the genus

It is strange that no country name compares Snowdrops with bells for they are bell-like as they swing to and fro. How do they swing on those delicate threads which connect flower to stem. You'd think they would be torn off. But they can stand any gale that blows. They yield to the wind rather than oppose it. A tree may be blown down in the night but never a single Snowdrop head is blown off. Their strength is that they know when to give in. There is a moral in that somewhere.

➤ H. L. V. FLETCHER, *Popular Flowering Plants*, 1971

The last six I saw.

➤ JIM CROSS, owner of Environmentals, a Long Island, New York, nursery specializing in dwarf woody plants, when asked to identify his favorite plants

I have one gardening rule—when in doubt plant Geranium endressii. I have never known such an accomodating plant. It never seems out of place. Put it among the aristocrats and it is as dignified as they are, let it romp in a cottage garden and it becomes a simple maid in a print dress. There are flowers all through summer, and they don't disagree with anyone.

➤ MARGERY FISH, *An All the Year Garden*, 1958

Forsythia is pure joy. There is not an ounce not a glimmer of sadness or even *knowledge* in forsythia. Pure, undiluted, untouched joy.

➤ ANNE MORROW LINDBERGH, *Bring Me a Unicorn*, 1971

Are you acquainted with the primulinus hybrid—those dancing butterflies of the Gladiolus garden? What the birds and the bees are to the fields, woods and meadows, or what the gay racing rills are to the rugged slopes, the primulinus are to the planted garden and landscape. They are grace, elegance, and color. They are daintiness, refinement, and art.

— Everett Earle Standard, "Those Butterfly Flowers: The Primulinus Hybrids," *Gardeners' Chronicle*, July 1928

Most modern roses are worth less than the soil they are planted in. Screw up brightly coloured rubbish and pin it to dead bushes to obtain the same effect without the problem of aphids.

— Josephine Saxton, *Gardening Down a Rabbit Hole*, 1996

Fit for nothing but very extensive shrubberies, where seen from a distance, the sight may endure it.

— William Cobbett on the sunflower, *The English Gardener*, 1929

I can admire and enjoy most flowers, but just a few I positively dislike. Collarette dahlias and those superlatively double African marigolds that look like india rubber bath sponges offend me most of all. I dislike the cheap texture of godetias almost as much as I do the sinful magenta streaks and splotches that run in the blood of that family. I loath celosias equally with dyed pampas-grass; and coxcombs, and spotty, marbled, double balsams I should like to smash up with a coalhammer . . .

— E. A. Bowles, *My Garden in Summer*, 1914

The nastiest of all weeds is that sycophant—Dock, called also Herb Patience. When you grasp the strong-seeming stalk, it has no fibre, it melts away in a soft squash, leaving its root in the ground; even Nettles are pleasanter to touch.

— Anna Lea Merritt, *An Artists Garden*, 1908

Ferns

Once you develop an interest in hardy ferns they almost become an obsession. I try to resist that; after all, it can't be healthy to be obsessed. You're no longer master of your passions, and anyway other plants tend to become unfairly excluded.

— CHRISTOPHER LLOYD, *In My Garden*, 1994

Ferns are confident enough to dispense with flowers altogether. Form is all and, undistracted by color, you can settle to the engrossing business of finding them suitable partners.

— ANNA PAVORD, *The Border Book*, 1994

The bright colours of flowers are admired by [even] the least intellectual, but the beauty of form and textures of ferns requires a higher degree of mental perception and more intellect.

— 1858 English fern catalog

They are the very quintessence of the woods, whether they rise to form a classic urn like the great ostrich, or quiver on ebon stems like the lovely maiden-hair. The very name has a fresh, fragile sound in any language—*Filices, felci, fougeres, Farnens, ferns.*

— GEORGE H. ELLWANGER, *The Garden's Story*, 1889

Flowers

A flower is an educated weed.

— LUTHER BURBANK

The delicate droop of the petals standing out in relief is like the eyelid of a child.

— AUGUSTE RODIN

The contrast between a voluptuous flower and its thorn is curiously satisfying, as if there were a human need for a visible dichotomy between the spike and the bloom, making the latter seem all the more precious and desirable.

— MONTAGU DON, *The Sensuous Garden,* 1997

My theory is that the flowers, appreciating how hard I try, cannot bear to disappoint me and, therefore, bloom their hearts out in recognition of this devotion.

— MARTHA SMITH, *Beds I Have Known: Confessions of a Passionate Amateur Gardener,* 1990

Most people look at *Eucomis* and see the obvious: A pineapple, I picture an overdressed, out-of-fashion, but stately woman (she may even be a man dressed as a woman) who clearly enjoys the astonished stares she elicits.

— ADAM LEVINE, "Screaming Lily the Anti Wallflower," *Garden Design* magazine, April 1999

More than anything, I must have flowers, always, always.

— CLAUDE MONET

I would have liked to pick one, groped for it,
But white frost had covered and hidden from me
The white chrysanthemum.

— OSHIKOCHI NO MITSUNE, ninth-century Japanese poet

There is a streak of the puritan in me, which chides me that time spent on things which merely flower and possibly smell nice, are merely ornamental, is time frittered away.

— SUSAN HILL, *The Magic Apple Tree,* 1982

A morning glory at my window satisfies me more than the metaphysics of books.
━ WALT WHITMAN

I got me flowers to strew Thy way:
I got me boughs off many a tree:
But Thou wast up by break of day,
And brought'st Thy sweets along with Thee.
━ GEORGE HERBERT, Easter, 1633

So many are the social qualities of flowers that it would be a difficult task to enumerate them. We always feel welcome when, on entering a room, we find a display of flowers on the table. Where there are flowers about, the hostess appears glad, the children pleased, the very dog and cat are grateful for our arrival, the whole scene and all the personages seem more hearty, homely, and beautiful, because of the bewitching roses, and orchids and lilies and mignonette!
━ SHIRLEY HIBBERD, *Rustic Adornments for Homes of Taste*, 1856

To be overcome by the fragrance of flowers is a delectable form of defeat.
━ BEVERLEY NICHOLS, author of *Down the Garden Path*, 1932

It would seem that there is a definite place in the garden scheme of things for brightly coloured flowers that need no dead-heading, flower continuously from the end of May until late October, and grow no more than five inches in height. As far as I know, such a plant does not exist for our climatic conditions, and I wish that the plant breeders would turn their attentions to producing one and would leave the old-fashioned flowers alone.
━ LYS DE BRAY, *Cottage Garden Year*, 1983

A fair flower springs out of a dunghill.
━ American proverb

You raise flowers for a year; you see them for but ten days.
— Chinese proverb

People from a planet without flowers would think we must be mad with joy the whole time to have such things about us.
— Iris Murdoch, novelist (1919–)

The flower is the poetry of reproduction. It is an example of the eternal seductiveness of life.
— Jean Giraudoux, *The Enchanted*, 1933

There is that in the glance of a flower which may at times control the greatest of creation's braggart lords.
— John Muir, *A Thousand-Mile Walk to the Gulf*, 1916

To me the meanest flower that blows can give
Thoughts that do often lie too deep for tears.
— William Wordsworth, *Ode; Intimations of Immortality from Recollections of Early Childhood*, 1803

The annual Helianthus or Sunflower towers like a priest raising the monstrance over the lesser folk in prayer and strives to resemble the orb which he adores.
— Maurice Maeterlinck, *Old-fashioned Flowers*, 1905

Every blade of grass, each leaf, each separate floret and petal, is an inscription speaking of hope . . .
So that my hope becomes as broad as the horizon afar, reiterated by every leaf, sung on every bough, reflected in the gleam of every flower.
— Richard Jefferies, "The Pageant of Summer," *Longman's* magazine, June 1883

One morning, very early, before the sun was up,
I rose and found the shining dew on every buttercup;
But my lazy little shadow, like an arrant sleepy head,
Had stayed at home behind me and was fast asleep in bed.
— ROBERT LOUIS STEVENSON, *My Shadow, A Child's Garden of
Verses.*

We live in a world in which flowers are more beautiful and more
numerous than formerly; and perhaps we have the right to add that
the thoughts of men are more just and greedier of truth. . . . It
behooves us not to lose sight of any of the evidence that we are
mastering the nameless powers, that we are beginning to handle
some of the mysterious laws that govern the created, that we are
making our planet all our own, that we are adorning our stay and
gradually broadening the acreage of happiness and of beautiful life.
— MAURICE MAETERLINCK, *Old Fashioned Flowers*, 1905

Each beauteous flower,
Iris all hues, Roses, and Gessamin
Rear'd high thir flourisht heads between, and
    wrought
Mosaic; underfoot the Violet,
Crocus, and Hyacinth with rich inlay
Broider'd the ground, more colour'd then with stone
Of costliest Emblem.
— JOHN MILTON, *Paradise Lost*, 1667

The single is pretty, but the double is splendid.
— ROLAND GREEN, *Treatise*, 1828

Anemone

The anemones likewise or windflowers are so full of variety and so dainty, so pleasant and so delightsome flowers, that the sight of them doth enforce an earnest longing desire in the mind of anyone to be a possessor of some of them at the least. For without all doubt, this one kind of flower, so variable in colours, so differing in form (being almost as many sorts of them double as single), so plentiful in bearing flowers, and so durable in lasting, and also so easy both to preserve and to increase, is of itself alone most sufficient to furnish a garden with their flowers for almost half the year.

— JOHN PARKINSON, *Paradisi in Sole, Paradisus Terrestris*, 1629

Walking past the apple tree on the lawn, I came round the corner made by its truck and stopped short with delight—the Anemone blanda have suddenly burst into flower overnight, it would seem, for their bright blue flowers are a complete surprise.

— LYS DE BRAY, *Cottage Garden Year*, 1983

Crocus

I grow a bit bored with my garden as August ebbs, but the colchicums and crocus always rouse me. The waning of the year is melancholy, but the crocuses are like spring at one's feet.

— WILFRED BLUNT, *Of Flowers and a Village*, 1963

It is surprising how—even today—many gardeners think of crocuses only in terms of the fat, blowsy and ubiquitous Dutch Crocuses of early spring. The alpine gardener, however, thinks of them with pleasure as a supreme race whose wide open chalices appear as if by magic in September, and whose various species can prolong the flowering season throughout the long winter days and on into April.

— ROY C. ELLIOTT, *Alpine Gardening*, 1988

Daffodil

To watch the upthrust of a daffodil, to see it take form as a flower-to-be, to see the bud grow and take on the warmth of color—there is the very synthesis of spring.
— HAL BORLAND, *Hal Borland's Book of Days*

No poet that I know of has ever bothered to sing the praises of winter aconites or of Scilla siberica, and history discloses no mad financial speculation in glory-of-the-snow, no great fortunes swiftly made in acquiring a handful of grape-hyacinth bulbs. Among spring flowers, the poetry belongs to the daffodil, which Sophocles, Shakespeare, Herrick, Wodsworth, and Amy Lowell have all celebrated in their turn.
— ALLEN LACY, *Homeground: A Gardener's Miscellany*, 1984

Of all the floral catalogues, the most exquisitely tantalizing is the daffodil catalogue. The further you read, the deeper the gold . . .
— GEORGE H. ELLWANGER, *The Garden's Story*, 1889

A house with daffodils in it is a house lit up, whether or not the sun be shining outside. Daffodils in a green bowl—and let it snow if it will.
— A. A. MILNE

Dahlia

The Dahlia's first duty in life is to flaunt and to swagger and to carry gorgeous blooms well above its leaves, and on no account to hang its head.
— GERTRUDE JEKYLL, *Wood and Garden*, 1899

Looking at my dahlias one summer day, a friend whose taste runs to the small and impeccable said sadly, "You do like big conspicuous flowers, don't you?" She meant vulgar, and I am used to that.
— ELEANOR PERÉNYI, *Green Thoughts*, 1981

Dandelion

There is no plant that doesn't merit a second look. Take the dandelion for instance: pick a bunch of them in spring and stuff them so closely together that they form a brilliant yellow pincushion standing in a blue clay pot, and I defy anyone to say they look awful.

— MIRABEL OSLER, *A Breathe from Elsewhere*, 1998

What a wealth to country children are the dandelions with their hollow stalks, linked into chains day after day, with untiring eagerness, and with the downy balls.

"The schoolboy's clock in every town," which come as the flowers fall away, and which sometimes whiten the meadow by their profusion, til a strong gust arises, and scatters them far and wide! Away they float, each white plume bearing onwards the seed at its base, so beautifully balanced, that its motion is most graceful, and its destined place in the soil most surely reached.

— ANNE PRATT, botanical illustrator, 1889

The massacre of dandelions is a peculiarly satisfying occupation, a harmless and comforting outlet for the destructive element in our natures. It should be available as a safety valve for everybody. Last May, when the dandelions were at their height, we were visited by a friend whose father had just died; she was discordant and hurt, and life to her was unrhythmic. With visible release she dashed into the orchard to slash at the dandelions: as she destroyed them her discords were resolved. After two days of weed slaughtering her face was calm. The garden had healed her.

— CLARE LEIGHTON, *For Hedges*, 1935

You cannot forget if you would those golden kisses all over the cheeks of the meadow, queerly called "dandelions."

— HENRY WARD BEECHER, American clergyman (1813–1887)

Advice on dandelions: If you can't beat them, eat them.
— DR. JAMES DUKE, botanist

Then there's the dandelion, which is actually sold in fancy markets in the spring and can be eaten raw in salad or cooked like in escarole; the French like to doll it up with pork lardons. Martha Stewart makes wine out of the flowers. But before you rush out to devour your lawn, keep in mind that dandelion is highly diuretic, a fact that is reflected in the plant's French name, pissenlit—pee in bed!
— ABBY ADAMS, *The Gardener's Gripe Book*, 1995

Delphinium

Beloved by all gardeners, but grown well by only a few.
— *The Avant Gardener*, on delphiniums, July 1999

Foxglove

White foxglove, by an angle in the wall,
Secluded, tall,
No vulgar bees
Consult you, wondering
If such a dainty thing
Can give them ease.
Yet what was that? Sudden a breeze
From the far moorland sighed,
And you replied,
Quiv'ring a moment with a thrill
Sweet, but ineffable.
— T. E. BROWN, British poet (1830–1897), "White Foxglove"

The spot of the Foxglove is especially strange, because it draws the colour out of the tissue around it, as if it had been stung, and as if the central colour was really an inflamed spot, with paleness round.

— JOHN RUSKIN, *The Queen of the Air*, 1869

Hellebore

An angel, legend has it, took pity on a little shepherd girl who had nothing to give the Infant Jesus in his manger. The angel handed her a weed, but first transformed it into this beautiful flower of winter.

— ALLEN LACY, on the Christmas Rose, *Helleborus niger*, *The Gardener's Eye*, 1991

The Christmas Rose must, I think, be dear to every one with a heart for flowers. Its expression is so full of innocence and freshness—for it is not only human persons who have expressions on their faces—and then the charm of its myrtle-like stamens and clear-cut petals—snow clad to the touch—and its pretty way of half-hiding among the dark leaves—always ready to be found when sought—and always with so many blossoms than had been hoped for!

— E. V. BOYLE, *Days and Hours in a Garden*, 1884

Hollyhock

Is anything more charming in its way than an old-fashioned single hollyhock in its pink or white, or yellow, or purple flower, and the little pollen powdered tree springing up from the bottom of the corolla! A bee should be buzzing in it, for a bee is never so deliciously pavillioned as in the bell tent of the hollyhock.

— OLIVER WENDELL HOLMES, "Trowel Work," *The New York Times Magazine*, May 15, 1949

Hyacinth

It is not easy to love a hyacinth. Not easy to place them, with their stiff cylindrical spikes of closely packed florets and their brilliant palette of pink and blue and white. They seem to demand a formality, even a regimentation, of a sort largely absent from our gardens today.

— KATHERINE SWIFT, "The Smell of Blue Hyacinths," *Hortus*, Spring 1999

It was as if a cluster of grapes and a hive of honey had been distilled and pressed together into one small boss of celled and beaded blue.

— JOHN RUSKIN

If I had but two loaves of bread, I would sell one and buy hyacinths, for they would feed my soul.

— *The Koran*

Iris

My Siberians don't teeter and topple in a rainstorm, and their withered blossoms aren't especially abtrusive. They're as understated and elegant as their tall bearded cousins are over-done and tarted up. They're lovely when in bloom, of course and their erect, narrow foliage remains an attractive accent in the border all during the growing season—something spiky to punctuate the more rounded forms of phlox and hemerocallis in midsummer.

— ALLEN LACY, *Home Ground: A Gardener's Miscellany*, 1984

If I am lukewarm about the dahlia, I am red hot about the bearded iris. I like it without qualification, and would not be without it in the garden.

— KATHERINE S. WHITE, "Irises," in *My Favorite Plant* by Jamaica Kincaid, 1998

I will have no more tall bearded irises. The love affair has ended.
— ALLEN LACY, (1935–)

Lily

So extensive and beautiful is the genus Lilium, so varied in form, color, and periods of blossoming, that, like the daffodil, a garden might be made up composed of it alone. We readily concede its beauty; the next thing is to manage it.
— GEORGE H. ELLWANGER, *The Garden's Story*, 1889

Tis God's present to our gardens [Lilium regale, the regal lily]. Anybody might have found it, but—His whisper came to me.
— ERNEST HENRY WILSON, **nineteenth-century plant hunter, on his discovery in China**

Lyllies and Roses planted together will both smell the pleasanter.
— WILLIAM LANGHAM, **The Garden of Health, 1579**

The lily was created on the third day, early in the morning when the Almighty was especially full of good ideas.
— MICHAEL JEFFERSON-BROWN, *The Lily: For Garden, Patio and Display*, 1989

The wood Lillie or Lillie of the valley is a flour mervallous sweet, florishing especially in the spring time, and growing properly in woods, but chiefly in valeies and on the sides of hilles. But now for the great commoditie and use known (of the floure) the same of late yeares is brought and planted in gardens.
— THOMAS HYLL, *The Proffitable Arte of Gardening*, 1568

The Lilies are a high and haughty race, impatient of cultivation and incalculable of temper.
— REGINALD FARRER, *My Rock-Garden*, 1908

The Conval-Lilly or Lilly of the Valley is esteemed to have, of all others, the sweetest and most agreeable Perfume: not offensive or overbearing, even to those who are made uneasy with the Perfumes of other sweet scented Flowers.

— JOHN LAWRENCE, *The Flower Garden*, 1726

There can be little that binds us so closely in spirit to people who trod the earth centuries before our own time as the knowledge that they, too, experienced similiar wonder and delight in the lilies of the field. Those plants neither toil nor spin, but so firmly do they bind us to their fragile charms that I feel sure the custom of strewing coffins with flowers originated in the hope that departed spirits might be lured back to earth by their magnetism.

— DAWN MACLEOD, "An Essayist in the Garden: Naming Names," *Hortus*, Summer 1994

The Lily is an herbe with a white flower: and though the leaves of the flower be white, yet within shineth the likeness of golde. The Lily is next to the Rose in worthines and noblenes.

— BARTHOLOMACUS ANGELICUS, *De Proprietatibus Rerum*, 1492

The great white Lily, the old lord of the gardens, whose nobility dates back to that of the gods themselves; the immemorial Lily raises his ancient sceptre, august, inviolate, which creates around it a zone of chastity, silence and light.

— MAURICE MAETERLINCK, *Old-Fashioned Flowers*, 1905

In whose backpack, war canoe, or slave ship did such a beauty travel to get here?

— SUSAN BROWN, "Portrait of a Lily," *Green Prints*, Summer 1999

Marigold

Marigolds are bright and beautiful if, like cousins, you don't have too many of them at once.

— HENRY MITCHELL, *The Essential Earthman*, 1981

It is as sprightly as the daffodil, as colorful as the rose, as resolute as the zinnia, as delicate as the chrysanthemum, as aggressive as the petunia, as ubiquitous as the violet, and as stately as the snapdragon. It beguiles the senses and enobles the spirit of man.

. . . Since it is native to America, and nowhere else in the world, and common to every state in the Union, I present the American marigold for designation as the national floral emblem of our country.

⌐ EVERETT M. DIRKSEN, American political leader (1896–1969)

I would rather see a field of marigolds with its exuberance and vulgarity—so sensual!—than one little precious darling of a plant.

⌐ NANCY GOSLEE POWERS, garden designer, quoted in *Breaking Ground: Portraits of Ten Garden Designers* by Page Dickey, 1997

Orchid

Orchids are more accomplished at the sensuous side of life than any of us.

⌐ DIANA WELLS, "A Florid Affair," *Green Prints*, Winter 1999/2000

This flower is exquisite, a real beauty, and obnoxious. She lacks spontaneity; she requires a vase. But she is a splendid woman, there's no doubt about it. No denying, either, that she possesses nobility. The orchid is an epiphyte, that is, a flower which lives on the surface of another plant without deriving nutrition from it.

What I've said isn't true: I adore orchids.

⌐ CLARICE LISPECTOR, "Four Selections from Dictionary," *Discovering the World*, 1984

"I'll make your drab little house look like Donna Karan's Hampton hideaway," sniffs a snow white phalaenopsis.

⌐ KIM RADCLIFF, "An Addict Confesses," *Garden Design* magazine, August/September 1999

Orchidaceae does not, as a rule, mean much more than Cypripedium, as far as the gardener is concerned; for Orchis, Ophrys, and the others of this most haughty and noble race are unapproachable, intractable plants in cultivation unless they happen to have brought themselves there.

— REGINALD FARRER, *My Rock-Garden*, 1908

Peony

Long ago I learned that really to see peonies they should be so grown that one could sit near or actually beside them. So I sit now on this twenty-eighth day of June, the fragrance of countless mock-orange blossoms filling every air that blows and the most glorious flowers that we have for our gardens, bar none, close at hand on their respective plants.

— MRS. FRANCIS KING, *The Beginner's Garden*, 1927

[She] always looks like a well-dressed, well-shod, well-gloved girl of birth, breeding, and of equal good taste and good health; a girl who can swim, and skate, and ride, and play golf.

— ALICE MORSE EARLE, garden writer (1851–1911), on the peony

No garden can really be too small to hold a peony. Had I but four square feet of ground at my disposal, I would plant a peony in the center and proceed to worship.

— MRS. EDWARD HARDING, *Peonies in the Little Garden*, 1923

Phlox

Life without phlox is an error!

— KARL FOERSTER, garden writer (1874–1970)

That's what I should have done instead of transplanting phlox. Their roots are tough, and I could never find the proper place to put them, the proper fence to set them off. White phlox up against a white fence, it never worked. I should have painted the fence blue.

━ LOUISE ERDRICH, **American novelist (1954)**

Poppy

I have discovered that I am a felon. You may be too.

Anyone who grows that beautiful old poppy, *Papaver somniferum*, is breaking the law. Most of you probably know that, but don't care. Gardeners are independent sorts obeying natural laws.

━ ANNE RAVER, **on the opium poppy,** *Deep in the Green*, **1995**

We usually think of the Poppy as a coarse flower; but it is the most transparent and delicate of all the blossoms of the field. The rest, nearly all of them, depend on the texture of their surface for colour. But the Poppy is painted *glass;* it never glows so brightly as when the sun shines through it. Wherever it is seen, against the light or with the light, always it is a flame, and warms the wind like a blown ruby.

━ JOHN RUSKIN, *Proserpina*, **1875**

Suddenly I looked and there, like a blue panel dropped from heaven—a stream of blue poppies dazzling as sapphires in the pale light.

━ FRANK KINGDON WARD, *Assam Adventure*, **1941**

It is to all other garden flowers what a milk-white unicorn might be in a barnyard, and that it is the envy of gardeners the world over . . .

━ WAYNE WINTERROUD, **on the Himalayan blue poppy (***meconopsis betonici***)**

As ardently worked for and . . . as difficult to succeed with as the sorcerer's stone.

— RUSSELL PAGE, on the Himalayan blue poppy (*meconopsis betonici*)

Rose

Nobody ever said Marigold is a marigold is a marigold.

— THE AMERICAN ROSE SOCIETY, who successfully lobbied for the rose as the national flower in 1986

He who would have beautiful roses in his garden must have beautiful roses *in his heart*.

— SAMUEL REYNOLDS HOLE, rosarian, 1869

If you are willing to learn, the rose will teach you.

— CYNTHIA WESTCOTT

God made a little gentian;
It tried to be a rose.

— EMILY DICKINSON, "Fringed Gentian"

Somehow my heart always opens and shuts at roses.

— DOUGLAS JERROLD, "Mrs. Caudles Curtain Lectures," 1852

All others are varieties of roses, but this grand flower is the rose itself.

— LOUISA JOHNSON, on hybrid tea roses, *Every Lady Her Own Flower Gardener*, 1839

A red florist's rose which has saved more marriages than all the guidance counselors of the world put together.

— PETER BEALES, *Twentieth-Century Roses*, 1989, on the rose "Baccara"

Fashions in flowers change as regularly as they do in clothes and cars, and nurserymen are quick to dispose of last-year's-model tulips or hyacinths. But roses were, and are, another matter.
 ← THOMAS CHRISTOPHER, *In Search of Lost Roses*, 1989

Nor will the sweetest delight of gardens afford much comfort in sleep: wherein the dullness of that sense shakes hands with delectable odours: and though in the bed of Cleopatra, can hardly with any delight raise up the ghost of a rose.
 ← THOMAS BROWN, *The Garden of Cyrus*, 1658

Gather ye rosebuds while ye may,
Old Time is still a-flying:
And this same flower that smiles to-day,
To-morrow will be dying
 ← ROBERT HERRICK, "To the Virgins, to Make Much of Time," 1648

But, for Man's fault, then was the thorn,
Without the fragrant rose-bud, born:
but ne'er the rose without the thorn.
 ← ROBERT HERRICK, "The Rose," 1647

Essentially beautiful flowers on rather ugly sticks.
 ← RICHARD BISGROVE, garden writer, quoted in *The Transplanted Gardener* by Charles Elliott, 1995

Go lovely rose!
Tell her, that wastes her time and me,
That now she knows,
When I resemble her to thee,
How sweet and fair she seems to be.
 ← EDMUND WALLER, "Go, lovely rose!," 1645

Oh roses for the flush of youth,
And laurel for the perfect prime;
But pluck an ivy branch for me
Grown old before my time.
➤ CHRISTINA ROSSETTI, "Oh Roses for the Flush," 1862

I sometimes think that never blows so red
The Rose as where some buried Caesar bled
That every Hyacinth the Garden wears
Dropt in Her Lap from some once lovely Head.
➤ EDWARD FITZGERALD, "Rubaiyat of Omar Khayyam"

When I plan a mixed border with roses, I try to think as much in
terms of scent as shape and color.
➤ ANDREW SCHULMAN, "Enduring Species Roses," *Fine Gardening*,
January/February 2000

Love is a rose, but you better not pick it.
➤ NEIL YOUNG, songwriter (1945-)

Tulip

A strang and forraine flower.
➤ JOHN GERARD *Herball*, 1597

I have never been interested in and am incapable of writing about
the great hybrid, garden tulips. I do not mean to condemn them
or anything foolish like that; but one cannot be interested in every
kind of garden plant and that particular kind has never made any
real appeal to me whatsoever. But the botanical species tulips are
quite another matter.
➤ EDWARD HYAMS, *The Gardener's Bedside Book*, 1968

Who could not fall in love with the Cottage tulip "Magier" as it opens its buds in May? The petals are a soft milky-white splashed with purple around the edges. As the flower ages, which it does gracefully and well (a worthwhile attribute) the whole thing darkens and purple leaches out from the edges through the entire surface of the petals. It is a mesmerising performance.

— ANNA PAVORD, *The Tulip*, 1999

Monsters, frightful to look upon.

— HENRY VAN OOSTEN, *The Dutch Gardener*, 1703, on parrot tulips

2 loads of wheat; 4 loads of rye; 4 fat oxen; 8 fat pigs; 12 fat sheep; 2 hogsheads of wine; 4 barrells of butter; 1000 lb of cheese; a bed; a suit of clothes; a silver beaker—the whole valued at 2,500 florins.

— The above goods were exchanged for one bulb during the height of the tulip craze that gripped Europe in the 1630s, quoted in *The Vegetable Book* by Yann Lovelock, 1972

Been there. Done that. That's the way many of us feel about tulips.

— FRANZISKA REED HUXLEY, *Garden Design* magazine, April/May 1995

Clean as a lady
cool as glass
fresh without fragrance
the tulip was

— Humbert Wolfe (1885–1940)

Violet

That, which above all Others, yeelds the Sweetest Smell in the Aire, is the Violet; Specially the White-double Violet, which comes twice a Yeare.

— FRANCIS BACON, "Of Gardens," an essay, 1602

Violets are the Spring's chiefe flowers for beauty, smell and use.
— JOHN PARKINSON, *Paradisi in Sole, Paridusus Terrestris*, 1629

The phrase shrinking Violet is really an overworked oxymoron. Violets have not inherited their corner of the earth due to any intrinsic meekness.
— PETER BERNHARDT, *Wily Violets and Underground Orchids*, 1989

One violet is as sweet as an acre of them.
— MARY WEBB, *The Spring of Joy*, 1917

Good God, I forgot the violets!
— WALTER SAVAGE LANDOR (1775–1864), British poet and writer, having thrown the cook out of an open window onto the flower-bed below

Zinnia

Old maid of the garden.
— JOSEPH BRECK, on the zinnia, *The Flower Garden*, 1851

Personally I like them higgledly-piggledy, when they look like those pots of paint squeezed out upon the palette . . .
— VITA SACKVILLE-WEST, *Some Flowers*, 1937

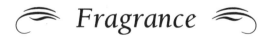

Fragrance

Honeysuckle has a fragrance that is reliably attractive, but you would be hard put to say exactly why, or even to describe it at all.
— MONTAGU DON, *The Sensuous Garden*, 1997

As the smell of hot leather to the huntsman, as the reek of a husband's old pipes to a widow, so is the incense of newly turned soil to a gardener in Spring. After a Winter of city reeks and the dismal stench of muddy roads in the gum-boot days of March and early April, go forth into your vegetable garden as a devotee into a church. Discard all the clothes the temperature and your proximity to neighbors will allow. Have the feet well booted. Drive the fork straight down till its tines disappear. Life the clod. Clout it. And around you arises the incense of the soil, which is better than all the perfumes of the East.
  ⬤ RICHARDSON WRIGHT, *The Gardener's Bed-Book*, 1929

A martyr to mildew.
  ⬤ NANCY STEEN, *The Charm of Old Roses*, 1987, on the scent of the rose "Jules Margottin"

Many escallonias are sticky and resinous, and at least two—illinita, and still more, viscosa—are said to smell of the pigsty; but to many people a good hearty smell of pig is not unpleasant, though perhaps out of place in a plant.
  ⬤ ALICE M. COATS, *Garden Shrubs and Their Histories*, 1964

The breath of flowers is far sweeter in the air where it comes and goes like the warbling of music, than in the hand.
  ⬤ FRANCIS BACON, "Of Gardens," 1625

Phloxes smell to me like a combination of pepper and pig-stye, most brooms of dirty, soapy bath-sponge, hawthorn of fish-shop, and meadow-sweet of curry powder . . .
  ⬤ E. A. Bowles, *My Garden in Summer*, 1914

Fragrance speaks more clearly to age than to youth. With the young, it may not pass much beyond the olfactory nerve, but with those who have started down the far side of the hill it reaches into the heart.
  ⬤ LOUISE BEEBE WILDER, *The Fragrant Path*, 1932

What is the best-smelling March flower? Why not ask what's the best cloud? Yet I am certain it is not the daffodil, which smells like a stale balloon.

— JIM NOLLMAN, *Why We Garden*, 1994

There was a smell of all the flowers at once, as if the earth had been unconscious all day and were now waking.

— BORIS PASTERNAK, *Doctor Zhivago*, 1958

The gift of perfume to a flower is a special grace like genius or like beauty, and never becomes common or cheap.

— JOHN BURROUGHS, **American naturalist (1837–1921)**

Certain flower scents imbibed when one is young are fixed unconsciously and indelibly in the psyche. Years later a smell of primroses, hawthorn, lilac or a certain rose may resurrect instant childhood.

— MIRABEL OSLER, *A Breathe from Elsewhere*, 1999

Flower lovers have been complaining for years that scent has vanished from the garden. Put your nose into a modern rose and sniff; most often, nothing at all happens.

— ABBY ADAMS, *The Gardener's Gripe Book*, 1995

The scents of plants are like unseen ghosts. They sneak upon you as you round a turn in the garden, before you can see the plants from which they came.

— BARBARA DAMROSCH, *Theme Gardens*, 1982

And the jessamine faint, and the sweet tuberose,
The sweetest flower for scent that blows.

— MARY SHELLEY, **"The Sensitive Plant,"** 1820

The Honisuckle that groweth wilde in every hedge, although it be very sweete, yet doe I not bring it into my garden, but let it reste in his owne place, to serve their senses that travell by it, or have not garden.

➥ JOHN PARKINSON, *Paradisi in Sole, Paradisus Terrestris*, 1629

Honeysuckle, whose scent represents the soul of the dew.

➥ MAURICE MAETERLINCK, *Old-Fashioned Flowers*, 1905

To the resuscitated noses is revealed the inimitable secrets of earth incense, the whole gamut of flower perfume, and other fragrant odors too intangible to be classed, odors which wing the spirit to realms our bodies are as yet too clumsy to inhabit.

➥ HANNA RION, *Let's Make a Flower Garden*, 1912

The tackroom smell of aromatic rhododendrons such as R. oreo-trephes, and most especially R. glaucophyllum, is unpleasant only to those whose childhood did not include shaggy ponies, neatsfoot oil and saddlesoap. The fronds of Acacia pravissima, when dried, smell very like the warm breath of horses.

➥ JANE TAYLOR, "Plants That Smell of Other Things," *Hortus*, 1989

One gardener's perfume is another gardener's stink.

➥ KATHERINE S. WHITE, *Onward and Upward in the Garden*, 1979

This tree is a pain in the nose.

➥ ANONYMOUS, on the California laurel

. . . the one smell that is more heart-racingly beautiful than the scent of any plant, and impossible to capture or contain within a garden, is the smell of warm, dusty soil immediately after a light shower of rain. The water releases an aroma of such fecundity that you almost expect growth to start erupting around you like time-lapse photography.

➥ MONTAGU DON, *The Sensuous Garden*, 1997

Chrysanthemums . . . smell of moths, camphor ball and drowned sailors.

—— SIR OSBERT SITWELL

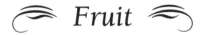 *Fruit*

Fine fruit is the flower of commodities. It is the most perfect union of the useful and the beautiful that the earth knows. . . . Trees full of soft foliage; blossoms fresh with spring beauty; and finally, fruit: rich bloom-dusted, melting and luscious; such are the treasures of the orchard and garden temptingly offered to every landholder in this bright, sunny, though temperate climate.

—— A. J. DOWNING, *Fruits and Fruit Trees of America*, 1845

In a sense the planting of fruit trees is a pledge of faith in the future, and even, perhaps especially, when the future is uncertain, it is important to make the gesture.

—— FRANCESCA GREENOAK, *Forgotten Fruit*, 1984

What wondrous life is this I lead?
Ripe apples drop about my head;
The luscious clusters of the vine
Upon my mouth do crush their wine;
The nectarine and curious peach
Into my hands themselves to reach.

—— ANDREW MARVELL, English poet (1621–1678)

For me, it would be perfect if the litchi had pretty flowers, and the peony bore good fruit.

—— CHANG CHAO, Yumengying, before 1693

In the morning, when I went to see how the garden had fared, there was a light fall of petals beneath the apple tree: there will not be so many apples this year perhaps, but I shall not mind because the plenitude that we so undeservedly enjoy is an embarrassment in autumn.

— LYS DE BRAY, *Cottage Garden Year*, 1983

The afternoon sun poured down on us through the drying grape leaves. The orchard seemed full of sun, like a cup, and we could smell the ripe apples on the trees.

— WILLA CATHER (1873–1947)

So it will be seen that a fruit tree is more beautiful than, for example, a sweet pea; for in the spring it is a little cloud anchored to the ground, in summer its branches are heavy with shapes carved of true jade, and in the autumn are weighed down with tinted and pleasant fruit. How dismal, as opposed to this excellence, enduring all the year, are the brown, tattered remnants of Michaelmas daisy and chrysanthemum.

— OSBERT SITWELL, *Penny Foolish*, 1935

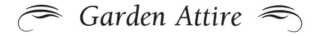

Garden Attire

From the size, weight and obvious service of these boots, it is evident to all who behold them that they were not chosen for appearances. This superb gardener always dressed in a manner that best served her work.

— RICHARDSON WRIGHT, describing Gertrude Jekyll's gardening boots, *Another Gardener's Bed-Book*, 1933

Gardens are places in which to fantasise. You can legitimately be Lord or Lady Muck for a while, and sometimes even dress up for the occasion. Try on straw hats in secret before going out in them, however, they can look very silly.

— JOSEPHINE SAXTON, *Gardening Down a Rabbit Hole*, 1996

Where are the sweaty face, the old clothes, the muddy-kneed pants (O. K., there is a charming picture of her [Martha Stewart] with muddy-kneed pants), the weeds, the bugs, the ravaged fingernails and the failed dreams that go into a real garden?

— ANNE RAVER, "Resolution: Next Year, Super Gardener," *The New York Times*, December 29, 1991

Of course, not all lovers of flowers can labor in the soil. Some of them haven't the right kind of shoes for it.

— LEONARD H. ROBBINS, *Cure It with a Garden*, 1933

No matter how cleaned up I am when they come in, my friends say they always see one to three *wet* shoes at the back door, evidence of my only just-stopped activity in the garden.

— HELEN VAN PELT WILSON, *Helen Van Pelt Wilson's Own Garden and Landscape Book*, 1973

In appearance great-aunt Lancilla was a very impressive old lady. . . . Under her skirt and fastened like an apron she wore a Pocket. . . .

A trowel and a small hand-fork, for instance, disappeared easily into those capacious depths, to say nothing of such trifles as stale bread for the ducks, corn for the pigeons, etc. Most people would find it difficult to walk gracefully with trowels and such knocking their ankles, but these impedimenta never seemed to interfere with her quick, yet dignified movements.

— ELEANOUR SINCLAIR ROHDE, *The Scented Garden*, 1931

⪦ *Garden Buildings* ⪧

Arguably, garden houses are not about gardening at all, since most keen gardeners would assert that there is never a moment in a gardening day when they would dare to sit down in one to ponder their activity.

— ROBIN WHALLEY, "Temples of Delight: An Exploration of Garden Buildings," *Hortus*, Spring 1999

Who loves a garden loves a green-house too.
Unconscious of a less propitious clime,
There blooms exotic beauty, warm and snug,
While the winds whistle and the snows descend.
The spiry myrtle with unwith'ring leaf
Shines there, and flourishes. The golden boast
Of Portugal and western India there,
The ruddier orange, and the paler lime,
Peep through their polish'd foliage at the storm,
And seem to smile at what they need not fear.
Th' amomum there with intermingling flow'rs
And cherries hangs her twigs. Geranium boasts
Her crimson honours, and the spangled beau,
Ficoides, glitters bright the winter long.
All plants, of ev'ry leaf, that can endure
The winter's frown, if screen'd from his shrewd bite,
Live there, and prosper . . .

— WILLIAM COWPER (1731–1800), "The Task"

The Potting Shed is the shrine of a ritual, a fertility cult, like the ceremonies connected with crops in tribal societies, with their Corn Maidens. It is the temple of a kind of magic. No wonder the uninitiated regard the Potting Shed with fear and fascination.

— HUGH POPHAM, *Gentlemen Peasants: A Gardener's ABC*, 1968

If everyone was given a greenhouse at birth he wouldn't dare to leave it for fear of the fire going out, and that would put an end to war.

⟶ CAPTAIN W. E. JOHNS, *My Garden*, March 1940

The architectural feature of all Unpleasaunces is the mysterious little *Shed* grey outside and black inside, which no one has the courage to explore on account of the peculiar and distressing smell which seems to be its only inhabitant.

⟶ W. C. SELLAR and R. J. Y EASTMAN, *Garden Rubbish & Other Country Bumps*, 1937

A greenhouse is a way of upgrading your hardiness zone.

⟶ HUGH JOHNSON, *Hugh Johnson's Gardening Companion*, 1996

 *Garden Catalogs*

Reading this literature is unlike any other reading experience. Too much goes on at once. I read for news, for driblets of knowledge, for aesthetic pleasure, and at the same time I am planning the future, and so I read in dream.

⟶ KATHERINE S. WHITE, *Onward and Upward in the Garden*, 1958, on garden catalogs

Warning: The Horticulture General has determined that opening this catalog may cause loss of mental and fiscal control.

⟶ From the cover of the catalog of The Plant Delights Nursery, North Carolina, owned by Tony Avent

As I write, snow is falling outside my Maine window, and indoors all around me half a hundred garden catalogues are in bloom.

⟶ KATHERINE S. WHITE

The dependents reverently produce the latest seed catalogue and succumb to mass hypnosis. "Look at those radishes—two feet long!" everyone marvels. . . . A list of staples is speedily drawn up. The children need a pumpkin for Halloween, and let's have plenty of beets, we can make our own lump sugar. Then someone discovers the hybrids—the onion crossed with a pepper or a new vanilla-flavored turnip that plays the "St. James Infirmary Blues." When the envelope is finally sealed, the savings account is a white sepulcher and all we need is a forty-mule team to haul the order from the depot.

— S. J. PERELMAN, *Acres and Pains*, 1943

Boy, what a flower! Red, and I mean RED! The brightest blood red you will find. This is not a blue-red or an orange-red but a hot red, red. Then to top it all off, it has a huge calyx which is nearly as large as the flower and you guessed it, bright red.

— Owner HAROLD GREER's catalog copy, *Greer Gardens*, Eugene, Oregon, on the rhododendron "Fireman Jeff"

We regard a very fat catalog as we do a very fat man—all the worse for its obesity.

— REVEREND HENRY WARD BEECHER, complaining about the "prodigal multiplication of varieties," including 61 different beans, in the William R. Prince catalog of 1842

Although you may enjoy dawdling over catalogs, it is wiser to select the best seedsman, send in your order—and go on to something else.

— RICHARDSON WRIGHT, *Another Gardener's Bed-Book*, 1933

"Light fragrance:" You have to crush it and shove it up your nose to notice.

"Provides winter interest:" Is stultifyingly boring the other three seasons.

"A challenge:" Will die.

"Spectacular:" Gaudy and tasteless.

— DUANE CAMPBELL, "Catalog Come-Ons: A Primer," *Green Prints*, Winter 1989/1990

I have grown wise, after many years of gardening, and no longer order recklessly from wildly alluring descriptions which make every annual sound easy to grow and as brilliant as a film star. I now know that gardening is not like that.

➤ VITA SACKVILLE-WEST, garden writer (1892–1962)

There are two seasonal diversions that can ease the bite of any winter. One is the January thaw. The other is the seed catalogues.

➤ HAL BORLAND, *The New York Times*, January 19, 1958

You must remember garden catalogues are as big liars as house-agents.

➤ RUMER GODDEN, *China Court*, 1961

Description is his best vein, however, and the adjective his staunch-est friend. Splendid, hardy, early, fine-flavored, pleasing, ornamental, mammoth, plentiful, profuse, enormously productive, smooth, symmetrical, improved, unrivalled, vigorous, abundant, royal—the catalogue man takes you to the happy planting grounds.

➤ WALTER B. HAYWARD, *The Commuter's Garden*, 1914

 *Garden Ornaments*

Rusty metal always looks very good with green foliage, so keep all broken or ancient tools, let them rust and make mobiles and assemblies in the borders.

➤ MONTAGU DON, *The Sensuous Garden*, 1997

I, for my part, doe not like Images Cut out in Juniper, or other Garden stuffe: They be for Children.

➤ FRANCIS BACON, "Of Gardens," an essay, 1602

A neighbor suggests that I might put up a scarecrow near the vines which would keep the birds away. I am doubtful about it: the birds are too much accustomed to seeing a person in poor clothes in the garden to care much for that.

— CHARLES DUDLEY WARNER, American essayist (1829–1900)

If you really and truly adore garden gnomes and reconstituted stone nightmares I still do not advise you to have them in a small garden.

— JOSEPHINE SAXTON, *Gardening Down a Rabbit Hole*, 1996

Here I have made the true Lover Knott. To try it in Mariage was never my Lott.

— STEPHEN BLAKE, *The Compleat Gardener's Practices*, 1664

A quick-set hog, shot up into a porcupine, by being forgot a week in rainy weather.

— ALEXANDER POPE, on topiary

Garden sculpture should mirror its environs. There is nothing wrong with pink flamingos or plaster gnomes, provided the garden is located in flamingo or gnome country.

— ROGER B. SWAIN, "A Christmas Goose," *Horticulture*, December 1985

I have always wished for a sun-dial in the middle of my grass walks where they widen into a circle. Even in an unpretending modern garden I do not think a sun-dial is affected, or, at any rate, not very . . .

— MRS. C. W. EARLE, *Pot-Pourri from a Surrey Garden*, 1897

It is with real sorrow that we see so many survivals of an era of not particularly good taste, in the shape of iron benches. It is their undoubted durability which has preserved them, and we who try to rest upon them are the sufferers, not only for their unpleasing appearance, but from the ill-chosen formation of the back . . .

— VISCOUNTESS WOLSELEY, *Gardens, Their Form and Design*, 1919

Too often, however, the return to formalism about the house was accompanied by the advent of hideous cement vases filled with lobelia and geraniums. In modern times gardeners have found more pleasing substitutes, such as terracotta vases and oil jars.

⟶ GERTRUDE JEKYLL, *Garden Ornament*, 1918

Keep some ornament in hiding, for your eyes only, tuck a pair of ceramic toads under the low hanging leaves of the ligularia. Set a brass heart in the baby's tears, where you'll see it when you weed. Scatter some glass beads in a frequently turned bed. . . . Position a statue in a nook behind the potting shed, where only you will visit. All will bring secret pleasure while you go about your garden labors.

⟶ LINDA SMITH, *Garden Ornament*, 1998

Nothing less than the gardener's certainty about the sculpture will ease the taunts he is likely to receive.

⟶ HENRY MITCHELL, upon acquiring a stone Chinese dog for his garden, *The Essential Earthman*, 1981

. . . what really sets my garden apart is the yard art my children and I love to scatter about—rusty garden implements, tire planters, gourd birdhouses and spoon wind chimes. Spray paint is our favorite medium. Nothing is sacred.

⟶ FELDER RUSHING, garden writer, "My Garden," *Garden Design* magazine, June/July 1995

I rarely sit here myself. It's really for family and friends. I try, but in two minutes I'm pulling a weed, pruning a twig, or giving something water. It's impossible for me to just *look* at my garden. If I'm near it, I want to be *in* it.

⟶ CYNTHIA WOODYARD, gardener, Portland, Oregon, quoted in *Horticulture*, March 1989, on garden seating

They stuck their ugly little painted terra-cotta faces out of frost-killed Funkia clumps. They leered at me beside a pool choked with leaves. They minced along a wall. And, to make matters worse, I was asked, "Don't you think they're cute?"

— RICHARDSON WRIGHT, on visiting a garden inhabited by gnomes, *Another Gardener's Bed-Book*, 1933

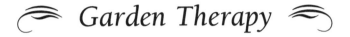 *Garden Therapy*

All my hurts
My garden spade can heal.

— RALPH WALDO EMERSON (1803–1882)

Gardening is a very calming, nonthreatening type of activity. Plants don't discriminate. They don't care if a person is 25 or 85, in a wheelchair or standing.

— JOEL FLAGLER, Rutgers University agricultural agent, on the benefits of gardening, *The New York Times*, August 12, 1990

Gardening is a complete therapy for all manner of blues, and for a lot of physical torments as well. Familiarise yourself with the principles of the wheel, the lever, and the big strong man, wear a body-belt around your lower back, take it slowly and learn to lift properly without exception.

— JOSEPHINE SAXTON, *Gardening Down a Rabbit Hole*, 1996

Why spend thousands studying with a guru on how to make your mind go blank when you can do the same thing for free lugging 50-pound root balls into the wheelbarrow?

— ANNE RAVER, "Tending the Gardener," *The New York Times*, June 21, 1992

Flowers . . . have a mysterious and subtle influence upon the feelings, not unlike some strains of music. They relax the tenseness of the mind. They dissolve its vigor.

➤ HENRY WARD BEECHER, American clergyman, (1813–1887)

Give me valium . . . or give me a garden.

➤ ANNE NELSON, "Give me Valium," *Green Prints*, Autumn 1993

They do not put a plant upside down. They have a deep natural sense of how plants grow.

➤ DR. OLIVER SACKS, neurologist, on deeply demented patients "who couldn't tell a knife from a fork" engaged in garden therapy

Garden Visitors

Won't you come into my garden? I would like my roses to see you.

➤ RICHARD SHERIDAN

Outside the wall of green made by tall spruces, I heard voices. One said: "Do look at those peonies—aren't they wonderful!" I called to the strangers, asking them to enter, to wander where they would. In they came, and we spent a few moments together enjoying the soft sight of many blooming flowers, the sweet scents in the dew, the rich greens of foliage and turf in the fading light; then I left them still exclaiming over the beauty of what they saw. But we had had together, these three unknown women and I that satisfaction of the common beauty of the common things of the common life; and such moments leave one happier.

➤ LOUISA YEOMANS KING, *Chronicles of the Garden*, 1925

If of this plant you don't see many,
Then be a good guy and don't pick any.
   — ANONYMOUS

When in the course of events the small estate has become too large
to be cared for by the residents alone, it is time to consider guests.
The guests, of course, have been around ever since you acquired a
place in the country, but until now they have been visitors. Putting
them to work should be easy.
   — ROGER B. SWAIN, *Field Days*, 1983

Visitors often tell me how much they love Barnsley [Barnsley
House, Gloucestershire, England] and how lucky I am to have such
a lovely garden. I must say it is not luck which makes the garden
lovely. It takes a tremendous lot of work—my staff of three or four
people work very hard to keep it in excellent trim, and I am in it
every day. When a garden is so much visited, one's standards simply can't relax. Gardens don't make themselves, and they certainly
don't keep themselves.
   — ROSEMARY VEREY, quoted in *The American Mixed Border* by Ann
    Lovejoy, 1993

You may ask isn't it a great nuisance for me to have a lot of people
around all the time?
   I like the people being here—they disturb me no more than the
birds twittering or the bees humming. You see, to create a garden
of this size and complexity and now fame, and allow nobody to
see it but a few friends, is exactly like writing a book and never
publishing it, or painting a picture and never exhibiting it. Apart
from that, if the people didn't come here, the place couldn't exist,
They pay for it.
   — NIGEL NICHOLSON, whose home, Sissinghurst Castle, receives
    125,000 visitors a year, quoted in *Horticulture*, July 1985

On first going unto a garden one knows by instinct, as a hound
scents the fox, if it is going to be interesting or not.
   — MRS. C. W. EARLE, garden writer, 1897

I cannot but think or dimly hope that horticulture has a code of ethics to itself. Why should a friend's seed-pod fall neglected, or a prey to slugs, when one has a pocket ready to receive it? However, I hasten to reassure all my acquaintances; my own spirit is far too meek for such adventures; I merely admire the law-breaker from afar. I cannot steal, though to beg I am by no means ashamed.

— REGINALD FARRER, *My Rock-Garden*, 1908

As soon as spring is in the air, Mr. Krippendorf and I begin an antiphonal chorus, like two frogs in neighboring ponds: What have you in bloom, I ask, and he answers from Ohio that there are hellebores in the woods, and crocuses and snowdrops and winter aconite. Then I tell him that in North Carolina the early daffodils are out but that the aconites are gone and the crocuses past their best.

— ELIZABETH LAWRENCE, *The Little Bulbs, a Tale of Two Gardens*, 1957

Things are always at their very best when I visit Mrs. M. Perhaps if I stayed a little longer, till dusk fell. I might detect a weariness among the lilies, the stocks might droop, and on her hard pavements I might catch the echo of rose-leaves falling. But I can never stay long at Mrs. M's. She annoys me too much.

— BEVERLEY NICHOLS, *Down the Garden Path*, 1932

. . . when Mr. Lock's or the Captain's gardeners favour our grounds with a visit, they commonly make known that all has been done wrong. Seeds are sowing in some parts when plants are running to seed while they are thought not yet at maturity. Our garden, therefore, is not yet quite the most profitable thing in the world. . . .

— FANNY BURNEY, *Diary and Letters*, 1794

I have been much afflicted again lately by visitors—not stray callers to be got rid of after a due administration of tea and things you are sorry afterwards that you said, but people staying in the house and not to be got rid of at all. All June was lost to me in this way, and it was from first to last a radiant month of heat and beauty; but a garden where you meet the people you saw at breakfast, and will see again at lunch and dinner, is not a place to be happy in.

— ELIZABETH VON ARNIM, *The Solitary Summer*, 1899

Gardeners

The chosen people of God.

— THOMAS JEFFERSON, on his fellow gardeners

Gardeners are famously pleased with themselves. They have excellent reason to be. Deep-rooted in the soil they stand like oaks, staunch in any furor, undisturbed by any gale of passion that blows. Under the strain of a blue Monday at the office or a black Friday on the Street, they think of the bed of English violets coming along beneath the dining room window, and thus they remain cool, calm and collected. It is not an axiom of business that amateur gardeners make the steadiest and safest of employees. It ought to be.

— LEONARD H. ROBBINS, *Cure It with a Garden*, 1933

Walter would not tolerate an unhealthy or badly grown plant and if he saw anything that wasn't looking happy he pulled it up. Often I would go out and find a row of sick looking plants laid out like a lot of dead rats.

— MARGERY FISH, *We Made a Garden*, 1956

Gardening is endlessly fascinating and diverse. Those of us who are irretrievably committed are immensely lucky. I am an enthusiast and I do believe that, numerous as the world's band of gardeners is, there should be more of us. Not just routine, but mad keen gardeners. Many lack the opportunity, but with others it's only a matter of finding the right person to start them off; someone prepared to communicate and share.

      ✎ CHRISTOPHER LLOYD, *The Adventurous Gardener*, 1983

Chance was to work in the garden, where he would care for plants and grasses and trees which grew there peacefully. He would be as one of them: quiet, open hearted in the sunshine and heavy when it rained.

      ✎ JERZY KOZINSKI, *Being There*, 1970

I find a real gardener is not a man who cultivates flowers; he is a man who cultivates the soil. He is a creature who digs himself into the earth, and leaves the sight of what is on it to us gaping good-for-nothings.

      ✎ KAREL CAPEK, *The Gardener's Year*, 1929

How lovely Aunt Dicksie's garden was. The ordering of her flowers was conceived in genius and by happy accident. Or was it accident? It was instead the essential beauty that was undefiled in her and unused, and by herself unrealised, finding here its right and only medium of expression. . . . Inch by inch and little by little, the stirring and unequal campaign in the garden absorbed more of Aunt Dicksie's energy and all her time and mind. She had at last in her life leisure to make gardening into a vice—a strange and lovely vice, a passionate ecstasy.

      ✎ MOLLY KEANE, *Mad Puppetstown*, 1932

I should like to enflame the whole world with my taste for gardening. There is no virtue that I would not attribute to the man who lives to project and execute gardens.

      ✎ PRINCE DE LIGNE, 1735

Gardeners are much worse than fishermen. Their arms stretch much wider when they are describing the height of their broad beans than when the fishermen are describing the length of a pike, and their tongues run away with them in a dreadful way, as though they were drunk with the scent of the flowers they were describing.

— BEVERLEY NICHOLS, English author (1898–1983)

And he gave it for his opinion, that whoever could make two ears of corn or two blades of grass to grow upon a spot of ground where only one grew before, would deserve better of mankind, and of more essential service to his country that the whole race of politicians put together.

— JONATHAN SWIFT, "A Voyage to Brobdingnag," *Gulliver's Travels*, 1726

Lyda was an exuberant even a dramatic gardener. . . . She was always holding up a lettuce or a bunch of radishes, with an air of resolute courage, as though she had shot them herself.

— RENATA ADLER, *Speedboat*, 1976

If the man who makes two blades of grass grow where one grew before deserves well of his fellows, surely he who turns plainness into beauty should be put upon a pedestal for worship, and, better still, for imitation.

— FREDERICK EDEN, *A Garden in Venice*, 1903

Out in the garden,
Out in the windy, swinging dark,
Under the trees and over the flower-beds,
Over the grass and under the hedge border,
Someone is sweeping, sweeping,
Some old gardener.
Out in the windy, swinging dark,
Someone is secretly putting in order,
Someone is creeping, creeping.

— KATHERINE MANSFIELD (1888–1923), "Out in the Garden"

Needless to say if I should fetch up in some dwelling without any garden at all, it would not bother me much. I began gardening with nasturtiums in my mother's discarded cold cream jars, and with sweet potatoes in a jar of water. And very satisfactory they were too. And are.

> ➤ HENRY MITCHELL, "A Garden in the City," *The Essential Earthman*, 1988

My method is to wait until some part of it annoys me and then take some action.

> ➤ HELEN DILLON, *Garden Artistry: Secrets of Designing and Planting a Small Garden*, 1995

There is life in the ground:
When it is stirred up, it goes into the man who stirs it.

> ➤ CHARLES DUDLEY WARNER, "The Love of Dirt," *My Summer in a Garden*, 1871

Gardeners have certainly arisen by culture and not by natural selection. If they had developed naturally they would look differently; they would have legs like beetles, so that they need not sit on their heels, and they would have wings, in the first place for their beauty, and secondly, so that they might float over the beds.

> ➤ KAREL CAPEK, *The Gardener's Year*, 1931

One of my pet hates is hearing people refer loftily to "real" gardeners as a mark of approval, as though there was such a think as an unreal gardener. There is no level of skill or performance by which to establish your rank as a gardener. It is a completely egalitarian activity. Gardeners are people who garden.

> ➤ MONTAGU DON, *The Sensuous Garden*, 1997

There is nothing mean in them, nothing but immense comradeship and fellow feeling, so that the learner is armoured from the start if he will take the trouble to ask questions fearlessly.

> ➤ MRS. MARION CRAN, *The Garden of Ignorance*, 1913

Are there not two sorts of gardeners? On the one hand are the lovers of colour: in their gardens you will find massed daffodils, tulip borders, colorful geraniums, delightful rose beds, and herbaceous borders that are their pride and joy. At the other extreme you have the gardener for whom modern phraseology has coined the word "plantsman." It is a noun covering both genders, and implies the sort of person who finds beauty in the old shrub roses, in quiet woodland plants, in shrubs whose beauty lies as much in their form as in their color.

➤ ROY C. ELLIOTT, *Alpine Gardening*, 1988

Like most gardeners, I have an abiding mistrust of progress. Synthetic fertilizers, turbo-charged tools and genetic engineering may fill agriculturists and extension agents with visions of utopia, but they are far less attractive to the practitioners of a craft that has not changed in its essentials since Pliny the Younger's slaves spelled out their master's name in boxwood hedges.

➤ THOMAS CHRISTOPHER, *In Search of Lost Roses*, 1989

In fact, the gardener is you and I, enraptured by a rose, enraged by an ant, entranced by a tomato, part-scientist, part-simpleton, and Mother Nature's midwife.

➤ HUGH POPHAM, *Gentlemen Peasants: A Gardener's ABC*, 1968

If I'm ever reborn, I want to be a gardener—there's too much to do for one lifetime!

➤ KARL FOERSTER, garden writer, plantsman (1874–1970)

 Gardening

I've never been without a garden. It's a lifetime challenge: a thing of beauty and a 3-D puzzle.

— BEATRICE J. ELYÉ, who has gardened for 50 years, passionate amateur award winner, *Garden Design* magazine December 1995/January 1996

Gardening is a ritual that responds to a desire in people to restore order. It says that everything is fine in the midst of chaos and bewilderment.

— BARBARA TUCHMAN, historian, quoted in "Paradise Found," *TIME* magazine, June 20, 1988

Gardening is not a rational act.

— MARGARET ATWOOD, "Unearthing Suite," *Bluebeard's Egg*, 1986

Uneventful living takes up most of our time. Gardening is part of it, possibly a trivial part to the rest of the world, but by no means less important to the gardener than the big events.

— GEOFFREY B. CHARLESWORTH, *A Gardener Obsessed*, 1994

So long as men are forced to dwell in log huts and follow the hunter's life, we must not be surprised at lynch law and the use of the bowie knife. But, when smiling lawns and tasteful cottages begin to embellish a country, we know that order and culture are established.

— ANDREW JACKSON DOWNING, landscape architect (1815–1852)

It's a joy that never fails.

— VISCOUNTESS WOLSELEY, *Gardens, Their Form and Design*, 1919

To make a garden is to organise all the elements present and add fresh ones.

— RUSSELL PAGE, garden designer (1906–1985)

Gardening is the only art form that works in four dimensions—
that is, the usual three, plus time. Time shapes the garden and
completes it; it also, in the end, destroys it.

— CHARLES ELLIOTT, *The Transplanted Gardener*, 1995

The great wonder in gardening is that so many plants live.

— CHRISTOPHER LLOYD, author of *The Well-Tempered Garden*, 1970

For me gardening is the greatest of all human achievements. Mi-
crochips, lasers, fiberoptics—these inventions pale beside the do-
mestication of plants.

Gardeners harvest the sun. Ours is an alchemy more precious
than turning lead into gold. We can turn sunlight into sugar.
Plants, of course, have been photosynthesizing without our help
for some 450 million years; we only learned to make the most of
it about 10,000 years ago. But no discovery before or since has
made such a difference.

— ROGER B. SWAIN, "Why I Garden," newsletter for WGBHTV,
Boston, Massachusetts

One of the greatest virtues of gardening is this perpetual renewal
of youth and spring, of promise of flower and fruit that can always
be read in the open book of the garden, by those with an eye to
see, and a mind to understand.

— E. A. BOWLES, *My Garden in Autumn and Winter*, 1915

Garden making, like gardening itself, concerns the relationship of
the human being to his natural surroundings.

— RUSSELL PAGE, *Education of a Gardener*, 1962

To make a great garden, one must have a great idea or a great
opportunity.

— SIR GEORGE SITWELL (1860–1943), *On the Making of Gardens*

A labour full of tranquility and satisfaction; natural and instructive, and such as (if any) contributes to the most serious contemplation, experience, health and longevity.

— JOHN EVELYN, *Kalendarium Hortense*, 1666

Gardening and Character

Among gardeners, enthusiasm and experience rarely exist in equal measures.

— ROGER B. SWAIN, author of *Groundwork: A Gardener's Ecology*, 1994

The garden, like beauty in landscape, is inimical to all evil passions: it stands for efficiency, for patience in labour, for strength in adversity, for the power to forgive.

— GEORGE SITWELL, *On the Making of Gardens*, 1909

The principle value of a private garden is not understood. It is not to give the possessor vegetables and fruit (that can be better and cheaper done by market-gardeners), but to teach him patience and philosophy, and the higher virtues—hope deferred and expectations blighted, leading directly to resignation, and sometimes to alienation. The garden thus becomes a moral agent, a test of character, as it was in the beginning. I shall keep this central truth in mind in these articles. I mean to have a moral garden, if it is not a productive one—one that shall teach, O my brothers! O my sisters! the great lessons of life.

— CHARLES DUDLEY WARNER, *My Summer in a Garden*, 1870

A weakness, found generally among advanced gardeners, is to scorn any flower easy of cultivation. The higher alpinists look down their noses at the lower alpinists who take delight in Creeping Phlox and Arabis. Rosarians of the 33 are not apt to have much sympathy with humble people who attain their horticultural ideals in Zinnias, Marigolds and Nasturtiums. And the exalted, esoteric air of the Lily-expert is proverbial.

— RICHARDSON WRIGHT, *Another Gardener's Bed-Book*, 1933

Patience is a flower that grows not in everyone's garden.

— **English proverb**

Learning gardening is learning about yourself so if you find yourself continually killing things, consider adding another activity to your life as well as gardening. This should be something needing controlled violence which does no harm, such as karate, clay pigeon shooting or cushion punching.

— JOSEPHINE SAXTON, *Gardening Down a Rabbit Hole*, 1996

Gardening is a lifelong philosophy which can be very humiliating. I put in $50 worth of tulips last fall and I got to see them for ten minutes before a storm smashed them. You have to be very tough to be a gardener. It's the antidote to narcissism.

— **PAMELA LORD, who consequently spent another $50 on tulips for the following year,** *Newsweek* **magazine, June 11, 1979**

Of the seven deadly sins, surely it is pride that most commonly afflicts the gardener.

— **MICHAEL POLLAN, author of** *Second Nature: A Gardener's Education*, **1991**

A love of flowers would beget early rising, industry, habits of close observation, and of reading.

— **HENRY WARD BEECHER, American clergyman (1813–1887)**

Judge men seldom, for it is a dangerous thing: when you do judge, seek first to behold him in his garden or in any other place which delights him and pleases in his heart.

— EDWARD COURSON, "Trowel Work," *The New York Times Magazine*, May 15, 1949

There is no gardening without humility. Nature is constantly sending even its oldest scholars to the bottom of the class for some egregious blunder.

— ALFRED AUSTIN, English poet, (1835–1913)

There's little risk in becoming overly proud of one's garden because gardening by its very nature is humbling. It has a way of keeping you on your knees.

— JoANN R. BARWICK, *Reader's Digest*, 1993

Nature thrives on patience, man on impatience.

— PAUL BOESE, *Reader's Digest*, September 1968

Gardening Books and Magazines

What another book of gardening! Are not our bookshelves already overburdened with literature on the subject?

— SAMUEL GRAVESON, *My Villa Garden*, 1915

The practical garden book is not a restful read. It eats at the conscience. It incites one immediately to weed.

— REBECCA RUPP, "Reading in the Garden," *Green Prints*, Summer 1990

Today I was plowing through a horticultural tome when I came to a chapter which began thus, "If you would rather have a really successful garden, it behooves you—" the hell it does. My garden is one place in the world where I am not behooved.

— JULIAN MEADE, *Bouquets and Bitters*, 1940

To the dismay of publishers everywhere, I believe that once you understand the basics, you are better off growing plants than reading about them. . . . The best advice that I have to give is to get out there and dig.

— ROGER B. SWAIN, *The Practical Gardener: A Guide to Breaking New Ground*, 1989

This is an identification guide to seedlings. It's for those of us who lose that quickly-soiled garden map almost immediately. No matter what you'd planned to sow there, or thought was sown there, these pages will tell you what *is* growing there.

— JUDITH ELDRIDGE, *Cabbage or Cauliflower?*, 1984

When a gardener has identified himself as the dirt variety he feels a marked superiority. But dirty fingernails are not the only requirement for growing plants. One must be as willing to study as to dig, for a knowledge of plants is acquired as much from books as experience.

— ELIZABETH LAWRENCE, *A Southern Garden*, 1942

Sometimes it can be disconcerting looking at pictures in gardening magazines, because they're always in full bloom; real gardens are always in transition.

— STEVE RANFT, Lexington, Kentucky, horticulturist

I will keep returning to the virtues of sharp and swift drainage, whether a plant prefers to be wet or dry. . . . I would have called this book Better Drains, but you would never have bought it or borrowed it for bedtime.

— ROBIN LANE FOX, *Better Gardening*, 1982

Books of Gardening are tedious; and difficult to be understood: and the best of them are very expensive.

➤ THOMAS PERFECT, *The Practice of Gardening*, 1759

It would require at least sixteen thick volumes bound in half calf, with bevelled edges, to contain a full account of a typical tour round any garden. There is so much history in every foot of soil.

➤ BEVERLEY NICHOLS, *Down the Garden Path*, 1932

It took me a long time to realize why my plan didn't work: the gardening magazines lie.

➤ AMY STEWART, "A Glamour Garden?" *Garden Prints*, Winter 1997/1998

Gardening, reading about gardening, and writing about gardening are all one; no one can garden alone.

➤ ELIZABETH LAWRENCE, *The Little Bulbs*, 1957

There are a few magnificent old gardening books written by learned scholars, but I think the majority of us love most those written by homely folk, who not only owned gardens, but worked there in themselves, for their books are redolent of the soil and of lifelong intimate friendship with plants.

➤ ELEANOUR ROHDE, *The Old English Gardening Books*, 1924

Numerous as are the books on gardening, and excellent as some of them undoubtedly are, there are many parts of the gardener's duty for which no general rules can possibly be laid down.

➤ PATRICK NEILL, *An Account of British Horticulture*, 1817

The garden is full of fairy stories; there is no end to them; it is not possible to go a yard from the door without meeting some new amusement, and every time I take up my pencil to try and write I feel confused by the mass of things I want to talk about, and more than half decide that it would be better to leave it all unwritten.

➤ MARION CRAN, *Joy of the Ground*, 1928

I have sometimes thought that the ideal gardening book has never been written, and I fear it never will be written. Its title should be "My Failures among Garden Plants," and it should deal exclusively with the adventures of a gardener of wide experience among the things he has failed in growing. There would be no reason why he should not tell of his successes when these have been preceded by disaster; but the main subject should be defeat, the facts and contributing causes. We should learn more by such a book than by any dozen of the exuberant publications that are nowadays so plentifully supplied us.

➤ HENRIETTA BATSON, *The Summer Garden of Pleasure*, 1908

If you choose to put it bluntly, I suppose that you could say that I wanted to put tall trees behind short trees, and light bushes against dark. But I do not choose to put it as bluntly as that. After all, I am writing this book, and so far, this book has not been at all blunt. It has whispered and rustled, and it will go on whispering and rustling . . . as long as I have anything to do with it.

➤ BEVERLEY NICHOLS, *Down the Garden Path*, 1932

The Garden as Evidence

My garden is an honest place. Every tree and every vine are incapable of concealment, and tell after two or three months exactly what sort of treatment they have had. The sower may mistake and sow his peas crookedly; the peas make no mistake, but come up and show his line.

➤ EMERSON's *Journal*, 1926

It is sometimes embarrassing that a garden is such an unbribable character witness to whoever planned and tended it. Our good taste, innate or acquired; our ignorance or experience; our energy or indolence are plainly set forth in our gardens . . .

— AGNES ROTHERY, *The Joyful Gardener*, 1927

Like the National Forests, my present garden is a multiple use facility. This garden is mixed in every sense of the word; not only are the borders full of all manner of plants, but the garden itself is the hub of our active family. It is as apt to host a horde of Cub Scouts as staid horticulturists, and is embellished with plastic wading pools rather than stately fountains. Several dogs and an embarrassing number of cats consider it their turf as well as mine.

The remarkable thing is that the garden often looks very nice despite all this, and that the heavy use results in surprisingly little damage to the garden or the gardener's temper. Because there is goodwill on all sides, the acre or so of garden satisfies most of its users most of the time.

— ANN LOVEJOY, *The American Mixed Border*, 1993

I began to feel more than anything in the world a garden betrays personality; it is a pitiless record . . . there is almost a feeling of invading privacy in coming in contact with a fresh one, the bias of its owner's mind is indicated, the range of his ideals, his perseverance or slackness in reaching them, his love of order, or disorder, his education, his breed, his nature, are laid bare to every eye; his very essence discovered.

— MRS. MARION CRAN, *The Garden of Ignorance*, 1913

The Garden as Sanctuary

A garden is a sanctuary as well as a creation. It increasingly becomes for me both a spiritual and a physical refuge more transforming than I'd ever imagined it to be. There is the particular kind of happiness—never commented on by poets—which comes from seeing that a shrub you'd once assumed dead, one day has minute specks of green on an otherwise lifeless stick.

— MIRABEL OSLER, *A Breathe from Elsewhere*, 1998

A garden is sort of sanctuary, a chamber roofed by heaven . . . to wander in, to cherish, to dream through undisturbed . . . a little pleasaunce of the soul, by whose wicket the world can be shut out.

— SIR ROBERT LORIMER, *On Scottish Gardens*, 1898

I like flowers very much, but cutting through everything, what I like best is the feeling when you step into a garden, that you've come out of the desert and here's a place dripping and steaming—a jungle, a Rousseauian landscape—something to sit in and look at where I can mull things over in my head.

— HENRY MITCHELL, quoted in "The Essential Earthman" by Barbara Seeber, *Horticulture*, April 1985

As for recreation, if a man be wearied with over-much study (for study is a weariness to the Flesh as Solomon by experience can tell you) there is no better place in the world to recreate himself than a Garden, there being no sense but may be delighted therein.

— WILLIAM COLES, *The Art of Simpling*, 1657

A place of enchantment in the mornings, where was felt the power of some subtle influence working behind bough and grass and birdsong.

— RICHARD JEFFERIES, *The Open Air*, 1885

 *The Garden at Night*

The garden, in the dark, allows for more primitive, secret response. If only the curious would keep their nagging to themselves.

➤ AUDREY COLOMBE, "Night Gardening," *Green Prints*, Winter 1993/1994

Why make an evening garden, a garden that doesn't awake until the twilight hours and, in many cases, is at its best long after the sun has set? The answer to that can be prefaced with another question: What's left of your day after you've met your commitments to family, home, job, and community?

➤ PETER LOEWER, *The Evening Garden: Flowers and Fragrance from Dusk til Dawn*, 1993

Since gardeners are quite mad and go prowling around their places at night . . . it isn't at all surprising to find that the mad ones plant flowers which are fragrant only at night.

➤ RICHARDSON WRIGHT, *The Gardener's Day Book*, 1938

The flower garden at night is an exotic spot, where an odor, a sound, or a light may signal an enemy, a meal, or a mate. It is virtually unexplored, though, for gardeners like other people are accustomed to daylight vision, and rarely go abroad in the dark without a streetlight or other artificial illumination. Instead they wait indoors imagining hordes of rabbits, woodchucks, and slugs rampaging through the shadows. But those willing to go on a sensual journey will venture into the garden after dark, receptive to the scents, sounds and sights of an unfamiliar place.

➤ ROGER B. SWAIN, *Earthly Pleasures*, 1981

The garden is so ferociously sexy at night, it's almost lurid.

➤ ANNE RAVER, on the lushly scented night-blooming flowers, *The New York Times*, August 7, 1984

White gardens are for the night; and the scent of the tobacco plant is unbelievable. Sometimes on hot nights I water the garden at two o'clock in the morning. You can't imagine how peaceful it is.

—ELIZABETH MACLEOD MATTHEWS, quoted in *The Passionate Gardener*, 1990

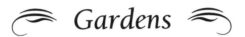

Gardens

Gardens, scholar say, are the first sign of commitment to a community. When people plant corn, they are saying, let's stay here. And by their connection to the land, they are connected to one another.

—ANNE RAVER, author of *Deep in the Green*, 1995

What is a garden but a species of desire?

—BONNIE MARRANCA, *American Garden Writing*, 1988

The gardens that bloom so beautifully in our minds, the ones where zinnias never die of wilt and summer days are never so hot that delicate leaves turn crisp and brown, these gardens are the Platonic ideal. The gardens we're actually stuck with, the ones where green beans drop before they're the size of matchsticks, corn plants topple in thunderstorms, and summer balsam germinates but never blooms, these gardens correspond to real life. This is the garden I have made, the garden where I must live. Its virtues are my own; its faults and limitations are mine, too. It exists at my forbearance, and without my constant attention, it will die—perish all the quicker because I garden in the desert, and if a garden is an expression of personality, it is just as much an expression of place.

—JANICE EMILY BOWERS, *A Full Life in a Small Place*, 1993

If you have a garden and a library, you have everything you need.
➤ MARCUS TULLIUS CICERO (106–43 B.C.)

A garden enclosed is my sister, my spouse, a spring shut up, a fountain sealed.

Thy plants are an orchard of pomegranates, with pleasant fruits; camphire, with spikenard,

Spikenard and saffron; calamus and cinnamon, with all trees of frankincense: myrrh and aloes, with all the chief spices:

A fountain of gardens, a well of living waters, and streams from Lebanon.

Awake, O north wind; and come, thou south; blow upon my garden, that the spices thereof may flow out. Let me beloved come into his garden, and eat his pleasant fruits.
➤ *The Bible,* Song of Solomon 4:12–16

This place before you is my reference library, regularly consulted with queries about nature. It also serves as a dance floor to court-ship rituals for countless species, including my own.
➤ From the yard brochure of Joy Buslaff, quoted in *The Avant Gardener,* July 1999

My garden is more of a problem than most because I expect it to be more beautiful every day in the year, and at the same time it must make room for plants that are new to me and may grow poorly or not at all. There are always a number of these, looking very forlorn until I make up my mind that they are not going to do better and might as well be discarded.
➤ ELIZABETH LAWRENCE, *Through the Garden Gate,* 1990

It is possible we will garden on American terms. We will make brave and beautiful gardens with hardier plants. And because we are a generous country, our gardens will be very generous and robust with a snap of the wilderness about them . . . perhaps aim-ing at what we lost.
➤ ROBERT DASH, painter

A garden, we say, should never compel us to go back the way we came; but in truth a garden should never compel us to do anything.
— GEORGE M. CABLE, *The Amateur Garden*, 1914

Obviously a garden is not the wilderness but an assembly of shapes, most of them living, that owes some share of its composition, its appearance, to human design and effort, human conventions and convenience, and the human pursuit of that elusive, indefinable harmony that we call beauty. It has a life of its own, an intricate, wilful, secret life, as any gardener knows. It is only the humans in it who think of it as a garden. But a garden is a relation, which is one of the countless reasons why it is never finished.
— W. S. MERWIN , "A Taste for Gardens," *House and Garden*, March 1997

For me, the garden is a place where things are simple, the two of us developing side by side. The world does not intrude here, judgments, egos are cast aside. Time zigzags, I am here and there, child and adult, guru and disciple at the same time. I may be by myself, but I am never alone. There is a whole community at my feet. The garden helps me to renew myself, scale down, evaluate what is truly important in life. The earthworm, that lowly life, teaches resilience. Life changes, it says, whether I submit or not. Here all creatures are truly equal, the scale is so large.
— LATHA VISWANATHAN, *Glimpse of Green: Women Writing on Gardens*, edited by Laurie Critchley, 1996

They are infinitely more numerous than the arriving stranger can suppose; they nestle with a charm all their own in the complications of most back views. Some of them are exquisite, many are large, and even the scrappiest have an artful understanding in the interest of color, with the waterways that edge their foundations. On the small canals in the hunt for amusement, they are the prettiest surprises of all. The tangle of plants and flowers crowds over the battered walls, the greenness makes an arrangement with the rosy sordid brick. Of all the reflected and liquefied things in Venice, and the number of these is countless, I think the lapping water loves them most. They are numerous on the Canalazzo, but wherever they occur they give a brush to the picture and in particular, it is easy to guess, give a sweetness to the house. Then the elements are complete—the trio of air and water and of things that grow.

━ HENRY JAMES, *Italian Hours*, 1909, on the gardens of Venice

People's backyards are much more interesting than their front gardens, and houses that back on to the railways are public benefactors.

━ JOHN BETJEMAN, *The Observer* (London) March 20, 1983

The real purpose of a back garden is to provide a place where a man can go and chop wood after he's had a row with his wife.

━ ANONYMOUS

Bad gardens copy, good gardens create, great gardens transcend. What all great gardens have in common are their ability to pull the sensitive view out of him or herself and into the garden, so completely that the separate self-sense disappears entirely, and at least for a brief moment one is ushered into a nondual and timeless awareness. A great garden, in other words, is mystical no matter what its actual content.

━ KEN WILBER, *Grace and Grit*, 1991

The turning circle of the garden year sometimes revolves all too quickly and sometimes slows almost at a standstill: the circle is like a coronet, gemmed at all times with jewels of different lustres and different colours, but all of them equally precious.

━ LYS DE BRAY, *Cottage Garden Year*, 1983

Unlike people, gardens never strive for perpetual youth—they want to look old from the day they were born. Their greatest glory comes with maturity.

━ THOMAS D. CHURCH, *Gardens Are for People*, 1955

A garden is an experience. It is not flowers, or plants of any kind. It is not flagstone, brick, grass or pebbles. It is not a barbecue, or a fiberglass screen. It is an experience. If it were possible to distill the essence of a garden, I think it would be the sense of being within something while still out of doors. That is the substance of it; for until you have that, you do not have a garden at all.
— JAMES ROSE, *Creative Gardens*, 1958

A house though otherwise beautiful, yet if it hath no Garden belonging to it is more like a prison than a house.
— WILLIAM COLES, *The Art of Simpling*, 1657

A garden is a *Gymnasium:* an outlet for energy, a place where accidents occur, where muscles develop and fat is shed.
— GEOFFREY B. CHARLESWORTH, *A Gardener Obsessed*, 1994

I judge a garden by the gardener who cares for it, the one who invests space with daydreams. How well I know the downward gaze into the face of the earth, the feeling of a luxurious body in good, dark soil that slips through the fingers in the rush to return to its dirty delirium. Each gardener creates an ideal world of miniature thoughts that drift languidly into each other like flowers on a dry afternoon. Here silence has the rhythm of wishes.
— BONNIE MARRANCA, *American Garden Writing*, 1988

# *Generosity/Greed*

Gardeners are generous with the ideas, even more so with their possessions. Visit a gardener and you will leave with your head full of ideas and your pockets brimming with cuttings and the like.
— THOMAS C. COOPER, "Gardeners Characteristics, " *Horticulture*, 1986

A very great part of the pleasure of gardening lies in the sharing of plants. Those people with the skill and knowledge to find and grow little-known plants have a responsibility to teach others, to pass on both information and plants. That's the only way heritage plants are preserved. Really this is the most important part of the freemasonry of gardening: give freely and you will also get.

➤ KEVIN NICOLAY, botanical artist, quoted in *Horticulture*, January 1990

I am not a greedy person except about flowers and plants, and then I am afraid I become fanatically greedy.

➤ MAY SARTON, American novelist (1912–)

Gardeners love to share . . . especially advice and cucumbers.

➤ TEXAS BIX BENDER, *Don't Throw in the Trowel*, 1996

Gardeners are generous because nature is generous to them, and because they know what it means to read about something and not to be able to get it.

➤ ELIZABETH LAWRENCE, *Gardening for Love: The Market Bulletins*, 1987

Every gardener knows this greed. I heard a man looking at a group of plants say "I have all the plants I need." Ridiculous. He said it because he was leaving for South America the next day, and he didn't have his checkbook, and it was December and he didn't have a coldframe.

➤ GEOFFREY B. CHARLESWORTH, *The Opinionated Gardener*, 1988

Of all hobbies, gardening is the least tainted with the jealousies one meets within the pursuit of other hobbies and recreations. It seems to make for generosity and good-fellowship the world over; and it is surprising how a total stranger will share his treasures with a kindred spirit, and to what trouble he will go to assist a fellow-gardener.

➤ ALICE MARTINEAU, *The Herbaceous Garden*, 1913

He is a bad gardener whose garden is kept only for himself.
　◟ CANON ELLACOMBE, *In a Gloucestershire Garden*, 1895

 *Gift Plants*

I am perplexed when some generous-hearted soul takes the trouble to dig up one of her favorite plants and lug it all the way to our garden as a present, the said plant being either a counterpart of a kind we have in abundance or a damned weed we have fought for years. Perhaps it might be set down, as one of the counsels of your garden perfection, to ask before you give.
　◟ RICHARDSON WRIGHT, *Another Gardener's Bed-Book*, 1933

When it looks ratty, don't try to stick it in the garden. It made you happy for a few weeks and that's enough; like a box of chocolates or a bottle of wine, you got the enjoyment, and now it's gone—that's enough satisfaction, isn't it?
　◟ EUGENE BAUER, La Crescent, Minnesota, nursery worker, on holiday gift plants, quoted in *Garden Smarts: A Bounty of Tips from America's Best Gardeners*, 1995

Pruning and cutting back are important skills in a small garden, especially as you have to bear constantly in mind the need to allow for the enhanced effects on growth of sun and rain confined to a small area. Arising naturally from this is another precept—something you must brace yourself to do—which is to discard temperamental or downright unsatisfactory doers. It is easy, but fatal, to give a year's stay of execution to a plant which is healthy enough, producing luxuriant greenery even in the poorest soil, but which sturdily refuses to earn its keep by flowering. Two years to get into its stride, three perhaps to be generous, but after that . . . a present to friends is my solution to the problem.
　◟ AUDREY DE LIÉVRE, author, 1981

Beware all exotic-seeming space fillers foisted onto you by well meaning people.

― JOSEPHINE SAXTON, *Gardening Down a Rabbit Hole*, 1996

 *Good Taste*

Certain gardens are described as retreats when they are really attacks.

― IAN HAMILTON FINLAY, English poet (1925–)

I love all the things most gardeners abhor!—moss in lawns, lichen on trees, more greenery than "colour," bare branches in winter. . . . I like the whole thing to be as wild as possible, to have to fight your way through in some places.

― EDNA WALLING, *A Gardener's Log*, 1948

Not all good gardens are shrines to good taste, but all are a place to be, welcoming the presence of people.

― ANN LOVEJOY, *The American Mixed Border*, 1993

The name *Poterium* caught my eye in a catalog, little knowing what leafy grace and odd flowering it had. These pink, mid-summer blooms look for all the world like miniature bottle brushes on wiry stems waving in the breeze. What a setback, then, to discover that *Poterium* is considered as "having no horticultural merit." However, there she flourishes, and there she stays!

― RICHARDSON WRIGHT, *Greedy Gardeners*, 1955

It has become fashionable to be old-fashioned in the garden.

― LEONARD H. ROBBINS, *Cure It with a Garden*, 1933

In truth, nothing can be more vulgar than my taste in flowers, for which I have a passion. I like any but the common ones. First and best I love violets, and primroses, and cowslips, and wood anemones, and the whole train of field flowers; then roses of every kind and colour, especially the great cabbage rose; then the blossoms of the lilac and laburnum, the horse-chestnut, the asters, the jasmine, and the honeysuckle; and to close the list, lilies of the valley, sweet peas, and the red pinks which are found in cottagers' gardens. This is my confession of faith.
> ← MARY RUSSELL MITFORD, from a letter to William Elford, April 17, 1812

You with your extraordinary taste have made it look like nobody's garden but your own. I think the secret of your gardening is simply that you have the courage to abolish ugly or unsuccessful flowers.
> ← HAROLD NICHOLSON, letter to Vita Sackville-West, 1937

The whole plantation, the garden, and the rest prove that a man born with natural taste may guess at beauty without having ever seen its model. The General has never left America; but when one sees his house and his home and his garden it seems as if he had copied the best samples of the grand old homesteads of England.
> ← A Polish visitor to Mount Vernon, June 1798

Style is a matter of taste, design a matter of principles.
> ← THOMAS CHURCH, *Gardens Are for People*, 1955

People are afraid they'll make mistakes. Who's to say what's good taste and bad taste? We're overly concerned with what's proper in plant selection—gardening is supposed to be recreation.
> ← ERIC LAUTZENHEISER, director, San Antonio Botanical Gardens, quoted in *Garden Smarts*, 1995

He has excellent taste and won't tell you something stupid. He's pigheaded, of course.
> ← HENRY MITCHELL quoted in "The Essential Earthman" by Barbara Seeber, *Horticulture*, April 1985, on Christopher Lloyd, one of his favorite gardening writers

They can be the most perfect flowers, but can also easily tip over that narrowest of dividing lines between splendour and absolute vulgarity. There are some hideous examples in the showier catalogues, violent orange and livid lemon, spotty or crudely streaked—as against delicately freckled.

　　━ SUSAN HILL, *The Magic Apple Tree: A Country Year*, 1982, on lilies

Any kind of riot—even in a garden—is bad taste. A riot presupposes lack of plan and lack of discipline and the garden that has neither thought in planning nor discipline in case should not be boasted about. Gardens are places of repose. Anything that tends to turn their orderly and gentle ways into a "riot" should be sternly repressed.

　　━ RICHARDSON WRIGHT, on the term "riots of color," *Another Gardener's Bed-Book*, 1933

Defect! Behave dangerously! . . . Why not go in for floral mutiny? Chuck out tastefulness, decorum, restraint, moderation and protocol and be outrageous with red hot pokers.

　　━ MIRABEL OSLER, *In the Eye of the Garden*, 1993

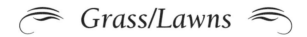

Grass/Lawns

Grass is the cheapest plant to install and the most expensive to maintain.

　　━ PAT HOWELL, landscape designer, Takoma Park, Maryland, quoted in *Garden Design* magazine November/December 1992

There's one good thing about snow, it makes your lawn look as nice as your neighbors.

　　━ CLYDE MOORE

Grasses endow our gardens with a wild and natural spirit. In the past, gardeners traditionally intervened powerfully and frequently—by cutting back, thinning, and removal—the minute foliage withered—and gardens were orderly, manicured, and tame. But by allowing plants to pass through the stages of seasonal metamorphosis, we now garden not tamely, but on the thrilling frontier between designed order and the full exuberance of nature. . . . Windblown, carefree, suggestive of prairies and country fields, grasses call to mind a younger, wilder landscape. Natural beauties, they belong in a nontoxic, good-looking, sophisticated, contemporary garden.

— CAROLE OTTESEN, *Ornamental Grasses: The Amber Wave*, 1990

What a thankless task it is to maintain a lawn! You've got to water it, feed it, and lime it so it will grow so well you have to cut it down the next week.

— CASSANDRA DANZ, *Mrs. Greenthumbs*, 1993

Grass is the hair of Mother Earth.

— KARL FOERSTER, garden writer (1874–1970)

Grass is indefatigible and indestructible. It will grow through tarmac, through concrete, through the soles of your boots, if you stand in the same place for more than about twenty minutes . . . There is, in fact, only one place where it is difficult, if not actually impossible, to get grass to grow and that is on those bare patches on the lawn.

— HUGH POPHAM, *Gentlemen Peasants: A Gardener's ABC*, 1968

I fought the lawn, and the lawn won.

— T-shirt logo

We love most the soft turf, which, beneath the flickering shadows of scattered trees, is thrown like a smooth natural carpet over the welling outline of the smiling earth. Grass, not grown into tall meadows, or wild bog tussocks, but softened and refined by the frequent touches of the patient mower.

— ANDREW JACKSON DOWNING, "Rural Essays," 1854

There is not a sprig of grass that shoots uninteresting to me.
— THOMAS JEFFERSON, letter to Martha Jefferson Randolph,
   December 23, 1790

I mow the lawn. How many people know the right way it should be done? Feet should be bare; grass should be slightly damp. The cold, moist clover strikes up from the mower upon my bare feet, and blades of cut grass and bits of slashed weeds stick between my toes.
— CLARE LEIGHTON, *Four Hedges*, 1935

Scientists have found that human beings prefer certain kinds of landscapes over others, and they theorize that this phenomenon shows our species' link to our ancestral home—the grasslands of Africa. When shown photographs of several landscapes and asked to choose which they preferred, people everywhere tended to choose grass landscapes. Maybe this inborn aesthetic sense explains our culture's fascination with the lawn.
— JEFF COX, *Creating a Garden for the Senses*, 1993

I believe a leaf of grass is no less than the journey-work of the stars.
— WALT WHITMAN

Grass is always the most elegant, more elegant than rocks and trees, trees are elegant and so are rocks but grass is more so.
— GERTRUDE STEIN, *The World Is Round*, 1939

Who can say that he ever saw a blade of grass come up out of the ground, much less that he ever saw one of the spears which survived the winter turn green? These things do nevertheless happen, and suddenly one is aware that they have happened.
— JOSEPH WOOD KRUTCH, *The Twelve Seasons*, 1949

He saw grasses. . . . They were varied kinds: fescues, rye grass, couch grass, meadow grass, hair grass, silky bent and quaking grass. They were silver-green, green-gold, pale and glassy, clear, new elm-leaf green and darker, bitter marshy-green. Fine lines down their stems glistened like stretched hairs: their finely swollen joints were glossy and shiny . . . they seemed almost impossible in their intricacy and difference one from another. Also beautiful.

━ A. S. BYATT, **English novelist (1936–)**

Herbs

There is no herb that is not medicine . . . what is rare is the man who knows how to put it to use.

━ **Sanskrit saying**

As I weed and cultivate the basils, savories, and thymes in my garden, touch their furry or glossy leaves, and breathe in their spicy scent, they seem like such old friends it is difficult to realize that only three years ago these aromatic herbs, except for the parsley, sages and mint, were quite unknown to me.

━ HELEN MORGENTHAU FOX, *Gardening with Herbs for Flavor and Fragrance*, **1970**

Camomile, the more it is trodden the faster it grows.

━ WILLIAM SHAKESPEARE

The many different scents that arise from the herbes, as cabbages, onions, etc., are scarce well pleasing to perfume the lodgings of any house.

━ JOHN PARKINSON, **on the placement of a kitchen garden, 1629**

As for Rosemarine, I lett it runne all over my garden walls.
— SIR THOMAS MORE

Herb gardening has been compared to chamber music. Both are
best appreciated in small places, for they have an intimate quality
lost in a large hall or in a big garden. Gardening with herbs, which
is becoming increasingly popular, is indulged in by those who like
subtlety in their plants in preference to brilliance.
— HELEN MORGANTHAU FOX, *The Years in My Herb Garden*, 1953

Tarragon is cherished in gardens. . . . Ruellius and such others
have reported many strange tales here of scarce worth noting, saying that the seede of flaxe put into a radish roote or sea onion, and
so set, doth bring forth this herbe tarragon.
— JOHN PARKINSON, *Paradisus terrestris*, 1629

The coleworts and all pot herbs are greatly defended from the
gnawing of the garden fleas, by radish growing among them.
— THOMAS HYLL, *The Gardener's Labyrinth*, 1577

Tarragon, sage, mint, savory, burnet—opening your pink flowers
at noon, to close three hours later—truly I love you for your-
selves—but I shan't fail to call on you for salads to go with boiled
leg of mutton, to season sauces; I shall exploit you.
— COLETTE, *Places*, 1971

As for the garden of mint, the very smell of it alone recovers and
refreshes our spirits, as the taste stirs up our appetite for meat.
— PLINY THE ELDER (23–79)

There is an irresistible urge in an herb garden to classify, sort, and
arrange all mints here; all sages there; all culinary herbs in one
corner; all medicinal herbs in another. This may suit the neat-
minded, but will not necessarily result in a good-looking display.
— ANNA PAVORD, *The Border Book*, 1994

When I pick or crush in my hand a twig of Bay, or brush against a bush of Rosemary, or tread upon a tuft of Thyme. . . . I feel that here is all that is best and purest and most refined, and nearest to poetry in the range of faculty of the sense of smell.

— GERTRUDE JEKYLL, **garden designer (1843–1932)**

Horticulture/Botany

The more I hear of Horticulture, the more I like plain gardening.

— JULIAN R. MEADE, *Bouquets & Bitters*, 1940

Horticulture is one pursuit of natural science in which all sexes and degrees of education and refinement unite. Nothing is too polished to see the beauty of flowers. Nothing too rough to be capable of enjoying them. It attracts, delights all. It seems to be a common field, where every degree of taste and refinement may unite, and find opportunities for their gratification.

— DANIEL WEBSTER (1782–1852)

You must not know too much, or be too precise or scientific about birds and trees and flowers and watercraft; a certain free margin, and even vagueness—

Perhaps ignorance, credulity—helps your enjoyment of these things.

— WALT WHITMAN (1819–1892)

Horticulture is sometimes described as a science, sometimes as an art, but the truth is that it is neither, although it partakes of both endeavors. It is more like falling in love, something that escapes all logic. There is a moment before one becomes a gardener, and a moment after—with a whole lifetime to keep on becoming a gardener.

— ALLEN LACY, *The Inviting Garden*, 1998

Botany is a lasting source of national amusement; and public utility.

━ "Preface," *Curtis's Botanical Magazine*, 1787

⪦ *Invasive Plants* ⪧

Some flourish for us, some hide their weed identity till networked into place. By then no spade uproots them. By then they have entered the language.

━ LOIS BEEBE HAYNA, "Seeds as They Fall"

Most weeds are just looking for a little place to call home. Crabgrass, on the other hand, has a hidden agenda. It is out to take over the world.

━ TEXAS BIX BENDER, writer (1949–)

Any healthy plant will develop shocking bad manners if left to itself.

━ FLETCHER STEELE, landscape architect (1885–1971)

The problem of an outside plant going inside is common to quaint old stone houses held together with ivy. One day you will discover a little vine sneaking along the top of the bookshelf, unusually because there is no house plant on the bookshelf.

━ DERECK WILLIAMSON, *The Complete Book of Pitfalls*, 1971

Ground covers are useful plants in their place, but one should be wary of any cataloque that promises that a ground cover will grow vigorously in any kind of soil, in sun or in shade, with no assistance from the gardener. There is another word for a plant like that: weed.

━ CASS PETERSON, *The New York Times*, November 29, 1992

Crabgrass can grow on bowling balls in airless rooms, and there is no known way to kill it that does not involve nuclear weapons.

— DAVE BARRY, **American humorist (1947–)**

When I first started gardening I used the ordinary bugle [Ajuga] in my flower-beds. It did the job very well, but had no idea when to stop. I have never met such an exuberant plant; it over-bugled everything, and I still find it trying to get another foothold in beds where I once grew it and from which it was banished—officially— many years ago.

— MARGERY FISH, *An All the Year Garden*, 1958

The total dimensions of the all-American ivy blanket that covers ground, fences, walls, tree trunks and lost tools and toys no doubt equal the acreage of Connecticut, add or subtract Rhode Island.

— GEORGE SCHENK, *The Complete Shade Gardener*, 1984

 *Knowledge*

All gardeners know better than other gardeners.

— Chinese proverb

Like many gardeners, I am rather a bungler. I know very little about pH soil tests. I think I know how to prune a rosebush, but the rosebush may think otherwise. I learned from my father the basic rules of mulching and thinning—how to stake out the tomatoes, how to make the peas climb up the chicken wire, how to bind up the raspberries—but the techniques that worked in the fertile hills of Vermont do not necessarily work in the sands of Long Island. Most important of all, I do not have the time (or the energy) to play some character out of Tolstoy. I live by the 8:26 to Penn Station, and most of the time, my roses grow untended.

— OTTO FRIEDRICH, "Of Apple Trees and Roses," *TIME* magazine,
  June 20, 1988

... a gardener's progress is best measured by the ability to learn what the plants already know.
➤ AURELIA SCOTT, "A Gardener's Progress," *Garden Design* magazine, July/August 1993

The education of a gardener is not a process that fits easily into a classroom or can be ferreted out of books during the falls and winters of four short years. It takes as many years as you have to give and then some. The reason, of course, is that formal knowledge is only a small ingredient of what is a complex concoction. Good gardeners, like their gardens, are distilled from a slow brew of long experience and personal alchemy.
➤ THOMAS C. COOPER, "A Note from the Editor," *Horticulture*, March 1985

Don't let beginner's luck give you delusions of knowledge.
➤ TEXAS BIX BENDER, *Don't Throw in the Trowel*, 1996

The more gardening you do, the better you get at it—you learn the tricks over a period of time. You have to have faith in yourself; even if you go to the books, common sense is the answer 90 percent of the time. You have to be persistent, have a little self-confidence, and keep plugging at it.
➤ JOHN KEHOE, greenhouse supervisor, Elizabeth Park Rose Garden, quoted in *Garden Smarts*, 1995

Study books, study gardens, and study wild nature, and use your own brains.
➤ HENRY ROBERTS, *The Book of Old-Fashioned Flowers*, 1901

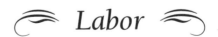

Labor

A garden is a thing of beauty and a job forever.
➤ ANONYMOUS

Are the people happier who are content to drift comfortably down the stream of life, to take things easily, not to *want* to take pains? . . . I only know that to my own mind and conscience pure idleness seems to me to be akin to folly . . . and that in some form or other I must obey the Divine command: "Work while ye have the light."
—— GERTRUDE JEKYLL, *Home and Garden*, 1900

Let us divide our labours, thou where choice
Leads thee, or where most needs whether to wind
The Woodbine round this Arbor, or direct
The clasping ivy where it climb, while I
In yonder Spring of Roses intermixt
With Myrtle, find what to redress till Noon . . .
—— JOHN MILTON, *Paradise Lost*, IX, 1667

People want their gardens to provide many pleasures, conveniences and comforts; none but dyed-in-the-wool gardeners want them to be any work.
—— THOMAS CHURCH, *Gardens Are for People*, 1955

To plow, to plant, to hoe, is the work which lies before us now.
—— *The Old Farmer's Almanac*, 1882

Did you ever meet a gardener, who, however fair his ground, was absolutely content and pleased? . . . Is there not always a tree to be felled or a bed to be turned? Does not somebody's ploughed field persist in obtruding its ugliness? Is there not ever some grand mistake to be remedied next summer?
—— DEAN HOLE, *A Book About Roses*, 1870

The secret of landscapes isn't creation. . . . It's maintenance.
—— MICHAEL DOLAN, "Public Works," *Garden Design* magazine, July/August 1992

Let us not have a garden of tiring care or a user up of precious time. That is not good citizenship. Neither let us have an old trousers, sun-bonnet, black finger-nails garden—especially if you are a woman.

— GEORGE M. CABLE, *The Amateur Garden*, 1914

Gardens are not made by sitting in the shade.

— RUDYARD KIPLING (1865–1936)

The best thing to put on a garden to make it grow is saline solution—the kind that comes off your face.

— WENDAL MITCHELL, Corbin, Kentucky

It is not graceful, and it makes one hot; but it is a blessed sort of work, and if Eve had had a spade in Paradise and known what to do with it, we should not have had all that sad business of the apple.

— COUNTESS VON ARNIM, *Elizabeth and Her German Garden*, 1898

The character-building part of the bed preparation.

— RITA PELEZAR, on removing sod, "The Last Leaf," *National Gardening* magazine, May/June 1994

The Gard'ners year is a circle as their labour, never at an end.

— JOHN REID, *The Scots Gard'ner*, 1683

Lazy/Casual Gardeners

There are those who conscientiously test their soil for acidity and eruditely compound their compost piles with chemicals. We have always tended to do so, but have not yet found the time for it.

We lime our vegetable garden when it looks sour, lime the limestone-fern bed each spring and fall if we remember it. . . . That is about as far as we ever get, and yet we have a pretty good garden.
— LEWIS GANNETT, *Cream Hill*, 1949

Sometimes the reader may be incited to exclaim: "What a lot of trouble!" or "Who wants to go through all that?" But however labour-saving you make your hobby, you will never get more out of it than you put in. Effort is only troublesome when you are bored.
— CHRISTOPHER LLOYD, *The Well-Tempered Garden*, 1997

I have taken to gardening a little, not a very inspiring business, though the strange debris of life which one turns up interest me.
— C. BENSON, **English poet (1862–1925)**

Fair-weather gardeners are to gardens what interior decorators are to buildings. They know only half the story. True gardening is as much about the bones of a garden as its planting; true architecture is as much about the form and structure of a building as its rooms.
— ROSEMARY VEREY, *The Garden in Winter*, 1989

I don't watch things grow. I pull them up. Only the weeds do much growing anyway, and my habits are not such that I could watch them even if I wanted to. When the sun and I come out, there they are—the size and shape of Miss Stephenson's delphiniums, but more muscular. It's a miracle, but I don't sing Te Deums about it.
— **Contributor's Club, "Watching Things Grow,"** *The Atlantic Monthly*, **July 1936**

Perhaps I shall give up any efforts to have a decent flowerbed. My heart is not really in it and the flowers know it.
— SUSAN HILL, *The Magic Apple Tree: A Country Year*, 1982

May I assure the gentleman who writes to me (quite often) from a Priory in Sussex that I am not the armchair, library-fireside gardener he evidently suspects, "never having performed any single act of gardening" myself, and that for the last forty years of my life I have broken my back, my finger-nails, and sometimes my heart, in the practical pursuit of my favourite occupation.
— VITA SACKVILLE-WEST, garden writer (1892–1962)

The fair-weather gardener, who will do nothing except when wind and weather and everything else are favourable, is never a master of his craft.
— CANON ELLACOMBE, *In a Gloucestershire Garden*, 1895

One of the nicest things about gardening is that if you put it off long enough it eventually is too late.
— BILL VAUGHN, "Trowel Work," *The New York Times Magazine*, May 15, 1949

 *Literary Gardeners*

In search of my mother's garden, I found my own.
— ALICE WALKER, *In Search of Our Mother's Gardens*, 1983

It is very difficult to write about flowers. I discovered this truth only when I started to do so. Before I tried my hand at it myself, I had done nothing but rail against those who were trying to do the same thing. I found myself losing my temper frequently with the nauseatingly sentimental phraseology which seems to impose itself on all those otherwise sincere and honest gardeners who feel impelled to transmit their knowledge and experience and emotions to other and more ignorant people. It seemed to me that they all employed the same sickly vocabulary, which deserved a dictionary to itself, so inevitable and recurrent were the terms they used. It is very difficult indeed to write about flowers.

— Vita Sackville-West, *Some Flowers*, 1937

I am writing in the garden. To write as one should of a garden one must write not outside it or merely somewhere near it, but in the garden.

— Frances Hodgson Burnett, *In the Garden*, 1925

I have grown further and further from my muse, and closer and closer to my post-hole digger.

— E. B. White, American author (1899–1985)

Garden writers are essentially comic writers, but we are always going to be more impressed by the heroic and the sublime. Yet in our dealings with nature at least, heroism and sublimity have probably run their course. To know when to laugh at nature, which will always be pulling the rug out from under us—will always, after all, have the last laugh—is part of wisdom.

— Michael Pollan, "A Gardener's Guide to Sex, Politics and Class War," *The New York Times*, July 21, 1991

It was one of the most bewitching sights in the world to observe a hill of beans thrusting aside the soil, or a row of early peas just peeping forth sufficiently to trace a line of delicate green. Later in the season the hummingbirds were attracted by the blossoms of a peculiar variety of bean; and they were a joy to me, those little spiritual visitants, for deigning to sip airy food out of my nectarcups. Multitudes of bees used to bury themselves in the yellow blossoms of the summer-squashes. This, too, was a deep satisfaction; although, when they had laden themselves with sweets, they flew away to some unknown hive, which would give back nothing in requital of what my garden had contributed. But I was glad to fling a benefaction upon the passing breeze with the certainty that somebody would profit by it, and that there would be a little more honey in the world to allay the sourness and bitterness which mankind is always complaining of. Yes, indeed; my life was the sweeter for that honey . . .

⇐ NATHANIEL HAWTHORNE, *Mosses from an Old Manse*, 1845

There is nothing pleasanter than spading when the ground is soft and damp.

⇐ JOHN STEINBECK (1902–1968)

All gardens are a form of autobiography.

⇐ ROBERT DASH

 *Lost Gardens*

If your garden was there before you were, chances are it grew out of many others' dreams.

⇐ FERRIS COOK, *Garden Dreams*, 1991

The sun shone down for nearly a week on the secret garden. The Secret Garden was what Mary called it when she was thinking of it. She liked the name, and she liked still more the feeling that when its beautiful old walls shut her in no one knew were she was. It seemed almost like being shut out of the world in some fairy place.

⇐ FRANCES HODGSON BURNETT, *The Secret Garden*, 1911

A garden really lives only in so far as it is an expression of faith, the embodiment of a hope and a song of praise.
— RUSSELL PAGE, *Education of a Gardener*, 1962

Then came the spring and the almost unbearable excitement, which can only be enjoyed in an ancient garden—of discovering where the previous owners had planted their bulbs. Of all the treasure hunts in which men have ever engaged, this must surely be the most enthralling . . . to wander out on a February morning, in an old garden which is all your own and yet is still a mystery, and to prowl about under the beech trees, gently raking away a layer of frozen leaves in the hope of finding a cluster of snowdrops . . . to scan the cold hard lawns in March for the first signs of the fresh green blades of the crocuses.
— BEVERLEY NICHOLS, *Merry Hall*, 1951

One of the rewards of buying an old house is the unexpected pleasure of uncovering the treasures which may be buried in the garden . . . full-grown boxwood hedges, and urns . . .
— THOMAS D. CHURCH, *Gardens Are for People*, 1955

Love

A man will talk of love out among the lilacs and roses, who would be stricken dumb by the demure propriety of the four walls of a drawing-room.
— ANTHONY TROLLOPE, *The Small House at Allington*, 1862

I began to fear that my intense love of a garden might be a mere hallucination, an idiosyncrasy, a want of manliness, a softening of the brain. Nevertheless I persevered in my inquiries, until I found that which I sought—the sympathy of an enthusiasm as hearty as

my own, a brotherhood and a sisterhood, who, amid all the ignorance and pretence of which I have given examples, were devoted
to the culture of flowers, and enjoyed from this occupation a large
portion of the happiness, which is the purest and the surest we can
know on earth, the happiness of Home.

➤ SAMUEL REYNOLDS HOLE, *Our Gardens*, 1899

Take it from us, it is utterly forbidden to be half-hearted about
Gardening. *You have got to LOVE your garden, whether you like it
or not.*

There is simply no literature, no help, and evidently no hope for
people who merely *like* having a garden, or don't mind if they do,
or fatalistically, just *have* a garden.

➤ W. C. SELLAR and R. J. Y EASTMAN, *Garden Rubbish & Other
Country Bumps*, 1937

Though truly determined lovers will meet almost anywhere, the
garden is their natural trysting place, just as it was for Romeo and
Juliet, Pyramus and Thisbe, Adam and Eve.

➤ BARBARA DAMROSCH, *Theme Gardens*, 1982

The first gathering of salads, radishes and herbs made me feel like
a mother about her baby—how could anything so beautiful be
mine?

➤ ALICE B. TOKLAS

The secrets are in the plants. To elicit them you have to love them
enough.

➤ GEORGE WASHINGTON CARVER (1864–1943)

Often I hear people say, "How do you make your plants flourish
like this?"as they admire the little flower patch I cultivate in the
summer, or the window gardens that bloom for me in the winter;
"I can never make my plants blossom like this! What is your secret?" And I answer with one word, "Love." For that includes all—
the patience that endures continual trial, the constancy that makes

perseverance possible, the power of foregoing ease of mind and body to minister to the necessities of the thing beloved, and the subtle bond of sympathy which is as important, if not more so, than all the rest. For though I cannot go so far as a witty friend of mine, who says that when he goes out to sit in the shade of his piazza, his wisteria vine leans toward him and lays her head on his shoulder, I am fully and intensely aware that plants are conscious of love and respond to it as they do to nothing else. You may give them all they need of food and drink and make the conditions of their existence as favorable as possible, and they may grow and bloom, but there is a certain ineffable something that will be missing if you do not love them, a delicate glory too spiritual to be caught and put into words.

— CELIA THAXTER, *An Island Garden*, 1895

The love of gardening is a seed that once sown never dies.

— GERTRUDE JEKYLL, garden designer (1843–1932)

There must be a heart gardener, as well as a head gardener, and you yourself must be the heart gardener: it is the heart gardener that makes a garden wherever plants will grow.

— ARTHUR HUMPHREYS, "Trowel Work," quoted in *The New York Times Magazine*, May 15, 1949

I have noticed the almost selfish passion for their flowers which old gardeners have, and their reluctance to part with a leaf or a blossom from their family. They love the flowers for themselves.

— CHARLES DUDLEY WARNER, American essayist (1829–1900)

To have "green fingers" or a "green thumb" is an old expression which describes the art of communicating the subtle energies of love to prosper a living plant.

— RUSSELL PAGE, *The Education of a Gardener*, 1962

Every time I go into a garden where the man or woman who owns it has a passionate love of the earth and of growing things, I find I have come home. In whatsoever land or clime or race, in whatsoever language, we speak a common tongue; the everlasting processes of earth bind us one, stronger than Leagues or Covenants can ever bind.
> ⌐ MARION CRAN, *How Does Your Garden Grow?*, 1935

A garden is not made in a year; indeed it is never made in the sense of finality. It grows, and with the labour of love should go on growing.
> ⌐ FREDERICK EDEN, *A Garden in Venice*, 1903

As a matter of fact, it was a love that appeared late in life, though all along it must have been within the man, for the instant he had a garden of his own the passion appeared full grown.
> ⌐ E. F. RUSSELL, *Garden Craft Old and New*, 1895

A good garden cannot be made by somebody who has not developed the capacity to know and to love growing things.
> ⌐ RUSSELL PAGE, *The Education of a Gardener*, 1962

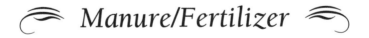

Manure/Fertilizer

I personally like manure. I never feel so affluent when bringing back the occasional load of high-class dung. When we moved here and I was preparing the new garden, Stu brought a pick-up load of horse manure as a garden-warming present. I never had a more welcome or thoughtful gift.
> ⌐ WILLIAM LONGGOOD, American journalist (1917–)

The fairest thing in nature, a flower, still has its roots in earth and manure.

— D. H. LAWRENCE (1885–1930)

When selecting land, do not be deceived by anyone who tells you that if not naturally good, the soil may be made so by cultivation and manure. These will help, certainly, but only as education improves the shallow mind. Luxuriant crops can no more be expected from a thin and poor soil—no matter how much it is cultivated—than fertile ideas from a shallow brain, educate it as you will.

— PETER HENDERSON, *Gardening for Profit*, 1874

We had a big flap with Ma Bell, but she finally decided to put us in the phone book. The first year we had to settle for Kricket?, the second, Kricket **XXXL!!!!, and this year, we got it: Kricket Krap.

— BILL BRICKER, describing the three-year process it took for the local telephone company to print the indelicate words of his product, quoted in "From Kitchen Waste Springs Garden Gold," by Anne Raver, *The New York Times*, November 21, 1991

It is said that hanging a scythe in a plum-tree, or an iron hoop, or horse shoes, will insure a crop of plums. This ought to be investigated.

— HENRY WARD BEECHER, American clergyman (1813–1887)

I used bag upon bag of finely shredded pig manure. . . . Emboldened by its obvious strength, I packed it in by the hundred-weight, three-fifths of pig manure to two-fifths of my heavy loam. You are not a gardener until you have untied a festering bag of this shredded manure and mixed it as top dressing. It gives my hands a temporary rash and my earthworms the excitement of a lifetime. Within weeks, shoals of long worms writhe in and out of its lumps, pink, fat and sleek like well-oiled Loch Ness monsters. For the first few days, keep the windows of your house firmly shut. The smell has that richness which lodges, like catarrh, halfway down your throat.

— ROBIN LANE FOX, *Better Gardening*, 1982

You should see the joy with which I gaze on manure heaps in which the eye of faith sees Delaware grapes and D'Angouleme pears, and all sorts of roses and posies.

— HARRIET BEECHER STOWE (1811–1896)

No poet I've ever heard of has written an ode to a load of manure. Somebody should, and I'm not trying to be funny.

— RUTH STOUT, *The Ruth Stout No-Work Garden Book*, 1971

"Llama beans" break down easily in the soil. And it's nicely piled for you, always in the same corner of the yard.

— DIANE CAVIS, llama breeder, quoted in *Garden Smarts*, 1995

Just remember the numbers 3-2-5. They refer to the three basic types—messy, stinky, and messy/stinky; the two sizes they are available in—tidbit (4-ounce packet) and blammo (220-pound sack); and the five methods of application—too much, too little, too early, too late, and wrong kind.

— HENRY BEARD and ROY McKIE, *Gardening: A Gardener's Dictionary*, 1982

A dear person, assisted by another dandy woman, gave me twenty-two plastic bags of horse manure for Christmas, and in last week's mild weather I got it spread on particular treasures in the garden. Ten roses on their arches had first claim, followed by the planting site of ten forthcoming tomato seedlings, then a dab for a crinum that should have bloomed in the summer but didn't, and a handful for the Princesse de Sagan (a red rose sitting all by herself), and a bucketful for what I hope is a hardy palm. Like youth, horse manure goes all too quickly. Before you've got started good, it's gone and you wonder how it went so fast.

— HENRY MITCHELL, *One Man's Garden*, 1992

"Putting on a little, anyway," of anything handy, particularly fertilizer, I found to be a habit that was hard to break, for like most people starting to garden it seemed to me that if a little was good, more of the same would be better. It isn't.

━ AMOS PETTINGILL, horticulturist (1900–1981)

Meditation

In the company of flowers we know happiness. In the company of trees we are able to "think"—they foster meditation.

━ JOHN STEWART COLLIS, "Farewell to the Wood," *Trees*, 1989

The most serious gardening I do would seem very strange to an onlooker, for it involves hours of walking around in circles, apparently doing nothing.

━ HELEN DILLON, *Garden Artistry*, 1995

I've noticed something about gardening. You set out to do one thing and pretty soon you're doing something else, which leads to some other thing, and so on. By the end of the day, you look at the shovel stuck in the half-dug rose bed and wonder what on earth you've been doing.

You've been gardening, an activity that doesn't necessarily lead directly to its supposed goal. This used to bother me, until I realized that this meandering—a kind of free association between earth, tools, body and mind—is the essence of gardening. What is supposed to be a practical, goal-oriented activity is actually an act of meditation.

━ ANNE RAVER, *Deep in the Green*, 1995

Here I am, weeding snipping and digging, and trying to work out the meaning of it all. I start at one end, and by the time I get to the other it's time to start again. It might seem a strange occupation. But people who think the mundane aspects of gardening are boring don't realise that repetitive garden tasks work like the repeated words of a mantra and free the mind to roam far and wide.

— Jo Munro, "A Sense of Place: What's a Garden, Anyway," *Hortus*, Spring 1999

There is probably nothing that has such tranquilizing effect, and leads into such content, as gardening. In half an hour I can hoe myself right away from this world.

— Charles Dudley Warner, *My Summer in a Garden*, 1871

You don't have to garden to garden; gardening in the mind is a gentle vice with an impetus of its own; it may not be as potent as actually making one, but there is a whole different threshold where gardening in the head can fill our winter tranquility with unrest. What gardener can condemn this as a time of stagnation?

— Mirabel Osler, *A Gentle Plea for Chaos*, 1989

Anyone who seeks that "peace which passeth all understanding" or, as the Buddists calls it, Nirvana, might well turn to his garden to distract his mind from the daily anxieties of life.

— Frank Kingdon Ward, *The Romance of Gardening*, 1935

Click, click, clickety, click. I introduce the shears to the grass. Click, click, clickety, click. Off with the heads of the wandering dandelion. Click, click, clickety, click.

With each blade of grass, a degree of the day's baggage slides from my shoulders to the ground. Click, click, clickety, click. My body and heartbeat begin to move to the rhythm of the shears. It takes about seven minutes to lose myself completely—which I do. After a particularly rough day, I even thought I hear the shears calling my name.

"Jean . . . Jean!"

Unfortunately, the voice was Sally's—my back-to-back neighbour.

I ignore her.

➤ JEAN BUFFONG, *Glimpse of Green: Women Writing on Gardens*, edited by Laurie Critchley, 1996

As I have gardened, feeling myself in some sort of deep dialogue with an unseen and silent partner, I have come to know true inner peace.

➤ MARTHA SMITH, *Beds I Have Known*, 1990

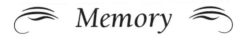 *Memory*

When you try to visualise this flowering society, when you call up all the flowers you can remember, and their tints and shapes and scents, the climates they like, the scenery they adorn, the memories they bring back, your mind begins to riot with flowering, and of all this colour and perfume and delight there seems no end or order.

➤ DONALD CULROSS PEATTIE, *Flowering Earth*, 1948

Scents bring memories, and many memories bring nostalgic pleasure. We would be wise to plan for this when we plant a garden.

➤ THALASSA CRUSO, *To Everything There Is a Season*, 1973

Yet other gardens exist, whose memory in secret cherished, is shrouded with a tender mystery. Lovelier than all gardens we have known, graced with the far-off charm of the unattainable are they, the gardens we have wished for, but have never seen. Words cannot paint them, yet the longing for them does still possess our hearts with visions of their beauty.

➤ E. V. BOYLE, *Seven Gardens and a Palace*, 1900

Beautiful things, perhaps, are never quite so perfectly beautiful as when they have passed beyond the untrustworthy criticism of eyesight into the safe guardianship of memory.

— REGINALD FARRER, *Among the Hills*, 1911

 *Mulch*

The only two herbicides we can recommend are cultivation and mulching.

— *Organic Gardening* magazine

I've been collecting bowling balls for a long time—people just throw them out.

— MARCIA DONAHUE, Berkeley, California, on her bowling ball mulch, quoted in *The Collector's Garden* by Ken Druse

Black plastic is not mulch; it is an abomination.

— SARA STEIN, *My Weeds: A Gardener's Botany*, 1988

When the United States Department of Agriculture starts mulching its tomato patch with a plant called hairy vetch instead of plastic, something is up: Organic gardening has gone mainstream.

— ANNE RAVER, "Now for Politically Correct Tomatoes: All Hail the Hairy Vetch," *The New York Times*, December 8, 1991

An unmulched garden looks to me like some naked thing which, for one reason or another, would be better off with a few clothes on.

— RUTH STOUT, *The Ruth Stout No-Work Garden Book*, 1971

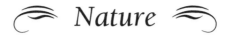 *Nature*

What nature has done for us is sublime and beautiful and unique.
— THOMAS JEFFERSON, letter to architect Robert Mills, 1811

The more you plan the more you set yourself up for disappointment. I let nature take her course and use gentle persuasion to get my way.
— SUSAN DUMAINE, gardener-botanist, quoted in "Susan's Garden," by John Barstow, *Horticulture*, April 1988

Nature to be commanded, must be obeyed.
— FRANCIS BACON, philosopher (1561–1626)

Gardening is always more or less a warfare against nature. It is true we do go over to the "other side" for a few hints, but we might as well abandon our spades and pitchforks as pretend that nature is everything and art nothing.
— JAMES SHIRLEY HIBBERD (1825–1890)

Nature writes, gardeners edit.
— ROGER B. SWAIN, *Groundwork: A Gardener's Ecology*, 1994

I do not know of a flowering plant that tastes good and is poisonous. Nature is not out to get you.
— EUELL GIBBONS, *Newsweek*, January 12, 1976

The sun, with all those plants revolving around it and dependent upon it, can still ripen a bunch of grapes as if it had nothing else in the universe to do.
— GALILEO (1564–1642)

Last night, there came a frost, which has done great damage to my garden. . . . It is sad that Nature will play such tricks with us poor mortals, inviting us with sunny smiles to confide in her, and then, when we are entirely within her power, striking us to the heart.

➤ NATHANIEL HAWTHORNE (1804–1864)

The majority of us gardeners in the earlier stages of our apprenticeship at times felt the irksomeness of long hours in the garden, the orchard, or the greenhouse, but were sustained and soothed by the magic influence of nature all around us.

➤ THOMAS A. CLARK, "The Spirit of Flowers," *Gardener's Chronicle*, May 1928

How the universe is like a bellows!
Empty, yet it gives a supply
that never fails;
The more it is worked, the more
it brings forth.

➤ LAO-TSU, Tao-te Ching, sixth century B.C.

That old thing. A romantic, but not entirely mythical notion, now discredited.

➤ HUGH POPHAM, on the balance of nature, *Gentleman Peasants: A Gardener's ABC*, 1968

The act of pollination is the foundation upon which civilization stands.

➤ MARIAN WILLIAMS, *Arboretum Leaves*, 1999

Nature does not hesitate to interfere with me, so I do not hesitate to tamper with it.

➤ HENRY MITCHELL, garden writer, 1923–1993

We still have a strong tendency to control our surroundings, but in our gardens we want plants, by their structure and poetry, to suggest the fine melancholy we expect in nature.

➤ THOMAS D. CHURCH, *Gardens Are for People*, 1955

"Flowers and trees," she said, "do not speak, but they do have hearts and spirits just like you and me. They can feel your love, hear your heart's message. And 'we' the guardians, were created to remind all things of their relationship, and to never forget Earth Mother. She is a living thing—very, very important in the Great Creation of the Great Spirit. Do you understand little girl?"

— TONY SHEARER, *The Praying Flute: Song of Mother Earth*, 1991

. . . nature is not to be copied—man cannot copy God's out-of-doors. He can only interpret its message in compositions of living tomes.

— JENS JENSEN, landscape designer (1860–1950)

Here Nature's Contrasts – Art attempts in vain;
Who can describe the joy that follows pain?
Or paint th'effect of sunshine after rain?

— HUMPHRY REPTON, "An Enquiry into the Changes of Taste in Landscape Gardening," 1816

Now I see secret the making of best persons. It is to grow in the open air, and to eat and sleep with the earth.

— WALT WHITMAN, *Leaves of Grass*, 1855–1892

Let me enjoy the earth no less
Because the all-enacting Might
That fashioned forth its lovliness
Had other aims than my delight.

— THOMAS HARDY, *Laughing Stocks and Other Verses*, 1909

This is the way the land is: up, down, straight across, undulating, an overcrowding that causes misshapenness (and the beauty of that is admired, but the patience to see it take shape is unbearable). To gaze on the land, to see the land for a great length of time will inspire the belief that the land has made us, has shaped us in a way that is only good; to gaze upon the land has made us, has shaped us in a way that is only good; to gaze upon the land, to see the land for a great length of time seems to inspire in us the desire to change the land, to make it into a shape that pleases us, to see it in a way that pleases us.

— JAMAICA KINCAID, *Poetics of Place*, 1998

Natural Gardens/ Native Plants

For the Heath, which was the Third Part of our Plot, I wish it to be framed, as much as may be, to a Naturall wildnesse. Trees I would have none of it; But some Thickets, made only of Sweet-Briar, and Honny-suckle, and some Wilde Vine amongst; And the Ground set with Violets, Strawberries, and Prime-Roses. And these to be in the Heath, here and there not in any Order.

— FRANCIS BACON, "Of Gardens," an essay, 1602

If you want to convert your lawn to a woodland, you are trying to compress a long evolutionary process into a few short years. You will have to make some compromises.

— ROSALIND CREASY, *Earthly Delights*, 1985

In the naturalistic garden, the site is king. It determines both the form and content of the garden. Topography determines the shape and even the placement of walks and paths, the lines of massed shrubs or trees, the forms of beds of herbaceous plants.

— HAL BRUCE, curator of plants at Winterthur, quoted in *Horticulture*, April 1985

If the only thing that moves in your backyard is a lawnmower, it's time to plant natives.

— JOY BUSLAFF, Wisconsin gardener, quoted in "Home Front Where the Wild Things Are?" by Rebecca Lowell, *The Wall Street Journal*, August 21, 1998

There are two reasons why I turned away from the formal style that employed foreign plants. The first reason was an increasing dissatisfaction with both the plants and the unyielding design—I suppose dissatisfaction with things as they are is always a fundamental cause of revolt—and the second was that I was becoming more and more appreciative of the beauty and decorative quality of the native flora of this country.

➤ JENS JENSEN, **landscape designer (1860–1950)**

Lovers of nature are curiously reluctant to admit that a completely natural garden is a contradiction in terms.

➤ ANNE SCOTT-JAMES, *The Pleasure Garden*, 1978

To have an environmentally correct native garden, it is not enough just to sit back and let the weeds grow tall; you must, it turns out, be as aggressive as though you were attempting a Versailles.

➤ ABBY ADAMS, *The Gardener's Gripe Book*, 1995

I never have to measure the pH of the soil or ask myself whether it is too wet or too dry for a particular species to do well. I don't have to worry about whether a plant is set too high or too low in the ground, whether its roots are damaged or potbound, whether or not it should be staked. I don't have to worry about hardiness or winterkill. And the price is always right.

➤ ROGER B. SWAIN, *Groundwork: A Gardener's Ecology*, 1994

Allow yourself to appreciate the awakening of nature and native plants, instead of getting lured in by rows of plants in black pots at the garden center.

➤ RICK DARKE, **curator of plants at Longwood Gardens in Pennsylvania,** *Garden Design* **magazine, April/May 1995**

The farmers, I find, think the mullein a mean unworthy weed, but I have grown to a fondness for it. Every object has its lesson, enclosing the suggestion of everything else—and lately I sometimes think all is concentrated for me in these hardy, yellow-flower'd weeds. As I come down the lane early in the morning, I pause before their soft wool-like fleece and stem and broad leaves, glittering with countless diamonds. Annually for three summers now, they and I have silently return'd together; as such long intervals I stand and sit among them, musing—wand woven with the rest, of so many hours and moods of partial rehabilitation—of my sane or sick spirit, here as near at peace as it can be.

    — WALT WHITMAN, "Mulleins and Mulleins," *Specimen Days*, 1882

If the extent and disposition of one's garden allows one to indulge in such luxuries as these little pockets of "regional gardening," how lucky one is! Half the secret of planting lies in happy association. Some plants "go" together; others, most definitely do not. There can be no rule, for it is essentially a question of taste and flair, but if a rule can be made at all it is that nature's own arrangements are usually best.

    — VITA SACKVILLE-WEST, *Some Flowers*, 1937

Landscaping is just being born, and its birthright is the soul of the out-of-doors. The world is rich in landscapes in harmony with soil and climatic conditions. In the virgin forest you can read the story of creation. There is no repetition, no over and over again, but there are a multitude of ideas for the fertile mind to work with and shape into something—that will inspire the race with a spiritual force for real accomplishments in the realm of art.

    — JENS JENSEN, landscape designer (1860–1950)

 *Neatness*

My trouble is that I was born a New Englander, and I must have things tidy. But as pleasure I think gardening ranks with spring house cleaning and Simonizing the car.

    — ANONYMOUS, Contributor's Club, "Watching Things Grow," *The Atlantic Monthly*, July 1936

A little, thin, flower border, round, neat, not gaudy.
  ← CHARLES LAMB, British essayist, 1806

I cannot lay too great stress upon the neatness in which a lady's garden should be kept. If it is not beautifully neat, it is nothing.
  ← MARIE E. JACKSON, *The Florist's Manual*, 1822

A garden given over to shapes, to straight-line paths, and boxwood hedges pampered into parallelepipeds, is a pitifully uninteresting representation of mathematical order.
  ← JEROME MALITZ, *Personal Landscapes*, 1984

There is last year's garden, lying all fallow and practically ready. Needs a little tidying up maybe—soggy newspapers . . . collapsed fences, the children's "clubhouse," a grape arbor that never saw a grape, a pile of ashes from the fireplace, and a completely strange rubbish barrel.
  ← C. B. PALMER, "Memoir Written with a Non-Green Thumb,
  The New York Times Magazine, June 12, 1949

 *Neglect*

Taking a vacation from the garden is a calculated risk. You know the best stuff will ripen while you're away, and if the racoons don't get it, the neighbors will.
  ← ANNE RAVER, *Deep in the Green*, 1995

I have a garden of my own,
But so with roses overgrown,
And lilies, that you would guess
To be a little wilderness.
  ← ANDREW MARVELL, English poet (1621–1678)

Weeds can be raised cheaper than most other crops, because they will bear more neglect. But they don't pay in the end. They are the little vices that beset plant life, and are to be got rid of the best way we know how. The first thing is to avoid getting their seeds into manure. It is almost as important to keep the manure, as to keep the land, clean. The next is to take them early. It is cheaper to nip them in the bud than to pull them up, root and branch, when they get ahead. Here is where the brainwork comes in. It is work that must be done.

— *The Old Farmer's Almanac*, 1881

Minor setbacks may be part of the rich tapestry of life in a garden, but at times the tapestry can appear a bit threadbare.

— MIRABEL OSLER, *A Breathe from Elsewhere*, 1998

When I returned to my garden, it had not been well cared for. A commercial "mow, blow, and go" gardener had come in and chopped the wonderful old rosemarys in half and pulled out all the lavenders and other precious wild things. He didn't know how to care for the old and wild. He didn't have a kind, loving relationship with them.

— ELIZABETH MURRAY, *Cultivating Sacred Space: Gardening for the Soul*, 1997

I couldn't get that voice out of my head. "Your leeks are late. Your leeks are late. You haven't even ordered your potatoes yet."

— ANNE RAVER, "Late Again," *Green Prints*, Winter 1995/1996

⚞ *Nongardeners* ⚟

I have met people who, through indifference or make-up, are by nature lethal to all forms of plant life. In spite of this, considerate planting and transplanting can be learnt and fingers and thumb trained to be more understanding.

— ZENIA FIELD, *Window-Box Gardening*, 1965

There are no green thumbs or black thumbs. There are only gardeners and non-gardeners.

— HENRY MITCHELL, *The Essential Earthman*, 1981

The modern [California] garden has been described as an informal outdoor living room filled with deck chairs, tables and swings, more social than horticultural in its intention.

— CHRISTOPHER GAMMP, "Gardens for California Living," *Landscape*, 1985

I don't dislike gardeners but I'd be just as pleased with them if they didn't go around trying to make me feel as if I hated nature. I don't hate it. I just don't like to grovel in the dirt.

— ANDY ROONEY, American humorist (1919–)

Nonweeders think we are odd but harmless. . . . Let 'em. They'll never know the adrenaline, the anguish, the chaos and carnage, the bloodbath that is a plant sale.

— KAY MELTZER, "The Battle of the Plant Sale," *Green Prints*, Spring 1999

I have a strong antipathy to everything connected with gardens, gardening and gardeners. . . . Gardening seems to me a kind of admission of defeat. . Man was made for better things than pruning his rose trees. The state of mind of the confirmed gardener seems to me as reprehensible as that of the confirmed alcoholic. Both have capitulated to the world. Both have become lotus eaters and drifters.

— COLIN WILSON, *A Book of Gardens*, 1963

"Why don't we keep it simple, this year—just some basil and a few tomatoes," my husband suggested. "We can buy everything else at the store."

— TERRI LU BENCAR, "Piggy, Tiggy, and Infinity," *Garden Prints*, Spring 1999

I'm afraid if I ever become a gardener . . . the world in general will become a never-ending source of danger.

— CALLIE VELMACHOS, "I am NOT a Gardener," *Garden Prints*, Summer 1999

Never trust a heavy drinker, who thinks that flowers are the splodges of colour in pub gardens, to water your plants when you are away for a few days.

— JOSEPHINE SAXTON, *Gardening Down a Rabbit Hole*, 1996

Novice Gardeners

If you have never gardened before, take heart. There is such a wide spectrum of horticultural temptations available that you're sure to get it wrong.

— MIRABEL OSLER, A Breathe from Elsewhere, 1998

For me it started with a house in the country and a new landscape, then learning the names of plants, buying them, too many, dividing them for friends, getting their surplus, looking at catalogues and going to nurseries, buying more plants, now old garden books, eventually finding myself in a garden too big to care for unless I quit my job. This, I think, is the general pattern of a gardener's life in its beginning stages.

— BONNIE MARRANCA, American Garden Writing, 1989

By mid-August of my first gardening year, when the entire office had been swamped by the floral deluge and I was reduced to putting bouquets on the desks of people I don't even particularly like, I began to feel like someone who had accessorized her clothing with a garlic necklace.

— MARTHA SMITH, *Beds I Have Known: Confessions of a Passionate Amateur Gardener*, 1997

If garden beginners knew in advance all the troubles in their way, they might never begin . . .

— LEONARD H. ROBBINS, *Cure It with a Garden*, 1933

"It isn't quite a dead garden," she cried out softly to herself. "Even if the roses are dead, there are other things alive."

She did not know anything about gardening, but the grass seemed so thick in some of the places where the green points were pushing their way through that she thought they did not seem to have room enough to grow. She searched about until she found a rather sharp piece of wood and knelt down and dug and weeded out the weeds and grass until she made nice little clear places around them.

"Now they look as if they could breathe," she said after she had finished with the first ones. "I am going to do ever so many more. I'll do all I can see. If I haven't time to-day I can come tomorrow."

— FRANCES HODGSON BURNETT, *The Secret Garden*, 1911

It astounds me still that I can succeed at gardening as though the growing of food and flowers should be so arcane that only an alchemist could carry it off. "Of course, I won't be very good at gardening. My garden won't look nice. It won't produce well." Those ideas were firmly in place at the beginning, and it's startling to find they're not true.

— JANICE EMILY BOWERS, *A Full Life in a Small Place*, 1993

Unlike that other type of virginity, you don't lose your horticultural innocence all at once.

— M. L. HARPER, "Horticultural Virginity," *Green Prints*, Autumn 1992

Less-experienced gardeners need the most help with the fortitude and resolve to thin.

⸺ RENEE SHEPHERD, Shepherd's Garden Seeds, quoted in *Garden Smarts*, 1995

Many people who love flowers and wish to do some practical gardening are at their wit's end to know what to do and how to begin. Like a person who is on skates for the first time, they feel that, what with the bright steel runners, and the slippery surface, and the sense of helplessness, there are more ways of tumbling about than of progressing safely in any one direction.

The real way is to try and learn a little from everybody and from every place. There is no royal road.

⸺ GERTRUDE JEKYLL, *Wood and Garden*, 1899

I have several acres about my house, which I call my garden, and which a skillful gardener would not know what to call.

⸺ JOSEPH ADDISON, *The Spectator*, September 6, 1712

Every man reaps what he sows—except the amateur gardener.

⸺ CHOLLY KNICKERBOCKER

Should you happen to come across me in the near future and hear me muttering things like "Sheep nesting high this year," "twill be a hard winter," or "Blossoms on bough, go milk a cow," or "i don't hold wi' all this manure on the land—tis against nature—give me Fisons every time," please evince no surprise. The fact is, I have acquired a window box and gone spectacularly horticultural overnight.

⸺ BERNARD LEVIN, *Taking Sides*, 1979

It is only the amateur [gardener] like myself who becomes obsessed and rejoices with a sadistic pleasure in weeds that are big and bad enough to pull, and at last, almost forgetting the flowers altogether, turns into a Reformer.

⸺ FREYA STARK, *Perseus in the Wind*, 1948

After the excitement of a beginner's garden, comes a lull. Many never pass that point. Dabblers and congenital amateurs, they are satisfied with their first experience. The work is too heavy. One blooming is enough for them.

— RICHARDSON WRIGHT, *Another Gardener's Bed-Book*, 1933

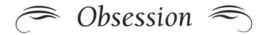

Obsession

You know you are a hard-core gardener if: you deadhead flowers in other people's gardens.

— SUE CARELESS, "A Horticultural Mania Quiz," *Fine Gardening*, August 1997

Never, in the history of the world, have so many men sacrificed so much, so often, at such a price, for so little. . . . There wasn't a night he wasn't hauling bags of manure and nitrogen, trimming around walks and trees on his hands and knees, watering, mulching and clipping. . . . Every new week there was some new gimmick to buy that sent everyone racing to the garden center.

— ERMA BOMBECK, *The Grass Is Always Greener Over the Septic Tank*, 1985

A garden is like those pernicious machineries which catch a man's coat-skirt or his hand, and draw in his arm, his leg, and his whole body to irresistible destruction.

— RALPH WALDO EMERSON (1803–1882)

I want everything. I have garden mania to an advanced degree.

— MARCIA DONAHUE, Berkeley, California, quoted in *The Collector's Garden* by Ken Druse, 1996

Color addicts who lurch incontinently from lumps of forsythia and double pink "Kanzan" cherries, through a blaze of rhododendrons and dumpy blobs of azaleas, floribunda roses, scarlet salvias, and so to a dying exit with mop-headed chrysanthemums.

— CHRISTOPHER LLOYD, quoted in *The Transplanted Gardener* by Charles Elliott, 1995

. . . no treatment or cure has been formulated for horticultural obsession. The best solution is to simply learn to live with it. Understand that, in warm-weather months, logical behavior will not be exhibited at or near your domicile. If your spouse brings home a six-pack of beer, it's for the garden slugs, not you.

— DAVID K. MILLER, "And Trowel, Do I Love Thee," *Fine Gardening*, May/June 1996

From January to April, my husband and children know where to find me. I'm in the basement with my seedlings.

— BONNIE MOSKOWITZ, Bayside, New York, passionate amateur award winner, *Garden Design* magazine, December 1995/ January 1996.

"You know," my brother said, as he was planning his plantings. "We've been cursed!"

— MARY CAROLWALL, on being a second-generation gardener, "Gardening: The Next Generation," *Garden Prints*, Autumn 1995

The trouble with gardening is that it does not remain an avocation. It becomes an obsession.

— PHYLLIS MCGINLEY, *The Province of the Heart*, 1959

If you are incapable of judging the time, if possible, get someone in the house to come and give you a gentle reminder. I had an aunt, a fanatical gardener, who came in one day soaked to the skin and said indignantly, "You *might* have told me it was raining."

— DOROTHY JACOB, *Flowers in the Garden*, 1968

You know you are a hard-core gardener if: you would turn down a job transfer to a city with a shorter growing season.

— SUE CARELESS, "A Horticultural Mania Quiz," *Fine Gardening*, August 1997

You have been warned. If you become seriously interested in plants then everything else will have less meaning. A life without holidays, sex, regular cooked meals and a trivial social life (i. e. other people not interested in plants) sustained snacks eaten with earthy hands and washed down with alcohol after sunset will enhance a life now filled with meaning.

— JOSEPHINE SAXTON, *Gardening Down a Rabbit Hole*, 1996

Ownership

When adolescence is passed the mind becomes, to a great extent, settled, and one acquires a bit of land of one's own. This is the beginning of your real garden, and it is then that gardeners are made.

— H. L. V. FLETCHER, *Purest Pleasure*, 1948

Gardens are a paradox. They reflect their owners; they are totally dependent; and yet in no time at all they are breathing with their own lungs, growing at their own pace, behaving with either willful disregard or subjugation. Subjugated gardens abound, and I can see why. Unless discipline is maintained from the moment the spirit-level is laid across the earth, you are nurturing a vast, tactile, heavy-scented siren which will keep you forever in its thrall.

— MIRABEL OSLER, "A Word about Boxes," *Hortus*, 1990

Broad acres are a patent of nobility; and no man but feels more of a man in the world if he have a bit of ground that he can call his own. However small it is on the surface, it is four thousand miles deep; and that is a very handsome property.

— CHARLES DUDLEY WARNER, *My Summer in a Garden*, 1870

All gardeners will know what I mean. Ownership makes all the difference in the world. I suppose it is like the difference between one's own baby and somebody else's. If it is your own baby you probably quite enjoy wiping its nose. If it is somebody else's you would have to use a long pole with a handkerchief on the end . . . at least I should.

— BEVERLEY NICHOLS, *Down the Garden Path*, 1932

When you are not concerned with their maintenance, gardens and the vagaries of their needs have a dreamlike quality which can never be recaptured once you know too much.

— MIRABEL OSLER, *A Breathe from Elsewhere*, 1999

His delight in his garden appears to arise more from the consciousness of possession than actual enjoyment of it.

— CHARLES DICKENS, *Sketches of Boz*, 1836

We trembled to remember those dark ages when we had loved the wild rose and the honeysuckle, when we had filled our small fists with violets, made golden balls of the cowslip, decked ourselves with daisy-chains, and when we were never weary of the tiny garden which was called our own.

— S. REYNOLDS HOLE, *A Book about the Garden*, 1909

⋐ *Paid Gardeners* ⋑

If you bee not able, nor willing to hyre a gardner, keepe your prof-
ites to your selfe, but then you must take all the paines.
 ➤ WILLIAM LAWSON, *A New Orchard and Garden*, 1618

Sow approximately 300 pots of poppies, 60 pots of sweet peas,
approximately 60 pots of white argemone and 30 yellow.
 . . . From the 15th to the 25th start the dahlias into growth.
Take cuttings from the shoots before my return; think about the
lily bulbs. If the peonies arrive, plant them immediately weather
permitting, taking care initially to protect the young shoots from
the sun. Do the pruning—don't leave the roses too long except for
the older thorny varieties.
 ➤ CLAUDE MONET's instructions to his head gardener Felix Bréuil,
 for the month of February 1900

An old lady's advice on choosing a gardener: "Look at his trousers.
If they're patched in the knees, you want him; if they're patched
in the seat, you don't."
 ➤ *Farmer's Journal*, Belfast, Northern Ireland

If anyone else helps you by doing your garden, then you have lost
it, even if you pay them a few hours a week, give up your career
and get down there yourself.
 ➤ JOSEPHINE SAXTON, *Gardening Down a Rabbit Hole*, 1996

If there is too much work, reflect on why heaven makes teenage
boys. If you stand there and direct the boys, they can do a passable
job for a modest amount of money.
 ➤ JEFF COX, *Creating a Garden for the Senses*, 1993

Well-trained gardeners who like their work must live in America, but not around here and not in my price range. When I look back on the long procession of incompetents, dumbbells and eccentrics, young and old, foreign and domestic, who have worked for me, I wonder how I and the garden have survived their ministrations.

It occurs to me that I attract the mentally unbalanced. Or perhaps their therapists have advised them to take up outdoor work?
— ELEANOR PERÉNYI, *Green Thoughts*, 1981

If paid labourers do some of the actual toil the honour will still belong to the selecting mind in command.
— MARY HAMPDEN, *Every Woman's Flower Garden*, 1915

A gardener is only helpful for the preliminary work of spading, after that his very presence is a profanation.
— HANNA RION, *Let's Make a Flower Garden*, 1912

So far as I can see, the only successful way to garden is to follow the Driscoll System, named for Neighbor Driscoll. He's got it down to an exact science and he always has a nice garden and enjoys every minute of it. His system calls for just three ingredients: an overstuffed garden chair, a shakerful of Martinis and a hired man.
— C. B. PALMER, "Memoir Written With a Non-Green Thumb," *The New York Times Magazine*, June 12, 1949

 *Pests and Disease*

The gardener has just as many allies as enemies among the fauna of his garden.
— HUGH JOHNSON, *Hugh Johnson's Gardening Companion*, 1996

When professionals do it, they call it "integrated pest management." But it's really just using common sense.
  ← KURT HASE, horticulturist, on using organic controls, quoted in "Weekend Journal," by Eileen White Reed, *The Wall Street Journal*, August 13, 1999

It is absurd to spray roses. I give them manure . . . reasonable attention. If they succumb to black spot, they can die and good riddance.
  ← HENRY MITCHELL, garden writer, 1923–1993

You should use a very light hand when it comes to pest control. Don't shop for the pest repellents that kill everything—because that's what they'll do, and that's no way to maintain a garden.
  ← ROGER B. SWAIN, "Weekend Journal," *The Wall Street Journal*, April 9, 1999

Pests aren't outlaws; they are constituents of ecosystems that thrive in response to our manipulations of those ecosystems, they will continue to respond favorably.
  ← DAVID RAINS WALLACE, *The Untamed Garden and Other Personal Essays*, 1986

In my garden goes a fiend
Dark and wild, whose name is Wind.
  ← GEOFFREY SCOTT (1885–1929)

There is nothing more unpleasant than to tell anyone suffering under a calamity that there is no tangible remedy; but it is infinitely better to do so than to delude them with a false one. I have been a worker of the soil since my boyhood, and every year's experience convinces me of the helplessness of remedies against insects or other blighting plagues that attack vegetation in the open field. It is true that the amateur gardener may save his dozen or two of cabbages or roses by daily picking off or destroying the insects but when it comes to broad acres, I much doubt if ever any remedy will be found to be practicable.
  ← PETER HENDERSON, *Gardening for Profit*, 1874

Gardeners wake screaming when they begin to think of the ghastly fate awaiting or overtaking their precious plants. The names alone read like something out of a manual for novitiate witches: Anthracnose, clubroot, Downy Mildew, Mites, Septoria, White Rot . . .

━ HUGH POPHAM, *Gentleman Peasants: A Gardener's ABC*, 1968

The garden free from pests, diseases and weeds is the garden of an unattainable Utopia. Nothing so reminds us that we are but one factor in a whole complex of ecological influences as when our plants suffer at the expense of some other organism, be it animal, vegetable, fungal, bacterial or viral.

━ STEFAN BUCZACKI, *Understanding Your Garden*, 1990

(*See also* Animals in the Garden)

Insects

You'll have to find the insect pests in your garden before you can identify them.

━ *Rodale's Chemical Free Yard and Garden*, 1991

These are the most mischievous things. They are wholly insensible to the powers of lime: in heat they delight: wet will not injure them; frost is their only destroyer; and many a time have I prayed for winter in order to see an end to caterpillars.

━ WILLIAM COBBETT, *Cobbett's Country Book*, 1975

The striped bug has come, the saddest of the year. He is a moral double-ender, ironclad at that. He is unpleasant in two ways. He burrows into the ground so you cannot find him, and he flies away so you cannot catch him. He is rather handsome, as bugs go, but utterly dastardly, in that he gnaws the stem of the plant close to the ground, and ruins it without any apparent advantage to himself.

━ CHARLES DUDLEY WARNER, *My Summer in a Garden*, 1871

Every insect has a mortal enemy. Cultivate that enemy and he will do your work for you.

━ ELEANOR PERÉNYI, *Green Thoughts: A Writer in the Garden,* 1981

Ants are a bit of a pest in their own right, quite apart from being both swottish and boring—always lugging things about that are too heavy for them, in that persistent servile way they have. If only, just occasionally, one of them would shrug its shoulders and walk off.

━ HUGH POPHAM, *Gentleman Peasants: A Gardener's ABC,* 1968

Gardening in September is often sad work, tinged with remorse; and besides, there are still mosquitoes.

━ LEONARD H. ROBBINS, *Cure It with a Garden,* 1933

Slugs

These animals smell with their bodies, come equipped with more teeth than a shark, and can glide without difficulty over broken glass, propelled by the rhythmic contractions of a single muscular foot.

━ DAVID GEORGE GORDON, *Field Guide to the Slug,* 1995

It is well known that slugs love to party; just leave a beer bottle in the garden overnight if you want proof. Set it on its side near the infant lettuce, with a tablespoon or so of beer left in it (any more would be a waste of B-vitamin complex). You are sure to find a half dozen crocked and reeling gastropods whooping it up in the morning.

━ ANN LOVEJOY, *The Year in Bloom,* 1987

Early one July morning, before the heat got intense, I went outside to begin what was becoming a surprisingly enjoyable routine: toss any slugs I could find, pull the most obvious weeds, take several deep breaths of the faint alyssum and rose scent already drifting in the air, tour the garden to see how the plants were doing, appreciate the clear sky and thank the Lord I lived in Portland, where a garden didn't require much time or talent.

— MEG DESCAMP, *Slug Tossing and Other Adventures of a Reluctant Gardener*, 1998

Before I knew what to do to save my garden from slugs, I have stood at evening rejoicing over rows of fresh emerald leaves just springing in rich lines along the beds, and woke in the morning to find the whole space stripped of any sign of green, as blank as a board over which a carpenter's plane has passed.

— CELIA THAXTER, *An Island Garden*, 1895

Now, here in the Northwest, venomous snakes are not everyday fare, but another sinister and slimy character lurks beneath every leaf, waiting to attack the unsuspecting gardener. Anybody who has ever stepped barefoot on a large and squashy slug will immediately see both the charm and the application of this concept. Slug Boots. I like it.

— ANN LOVEJOY, garden writer (1951–)

We have descended into the garden and caught three hundred slugs. How I love the mixture of the beautiful and the squalid in gardening. It makes it so lifelike.

— EVELYN UNDERHILL, 1912, *The Letters of Evelyn Underhill*, 1943

 *Philosophy*

A garden which is a battleground against the less amiable and co-operative forces of nature can scarcely be a source of serenity. The gardener must be a philosopher, accepting that he and his have a place in the cycle of life which nothing or very little, can alter.
— HUGH JOHNSON, *Hugh Johnson's Gardening Companion*, 1996

The profit of the earth is for all.
— Ecclesiastes

To forget how to dig the earth and tend to the soil is to forget ourselves.
— MAHATMAS GANDHI (1869–1948)

If you would be happy for a week take a wife, if you would be happy for a month kill a pig; but if you would be happy all your life, plant a garden.
— Chinese proverb

To dwell is to garden.
— MARTIN HEIDEGGER (1889–1976)

More things grow in the garden than the gardener sows.
— Spanish proverb

As long as one has a garden one has a future; and as long as one has a future one is alive.
— FRANCES HODGSON BURNETT, *In the Garden*, 1925

When a man has found all the rest of the world vanity, he retires into his garden.
— ANONYMOUS

Fortune may smile on some but for the rest of us she just laughs.
— Gurney's spring catalog

We learn from our gardens to deal with the most urgent question of the time: How much is enough?
— WENDELL BERRY, American poet and nature writer (1934–)

Not every soil can bear all things.
— VIRGIL

Never forget:
We walk on hell
Gazing at flowers.
— ISSA, Japanese poet, 1763–1827

One grower's success may be another's waste of time.
— *The Encyclopedia of Natural Insect and Disease Control*, Rodale Press, 1984

Plant Names/ Taxonomy/Garden Terminology

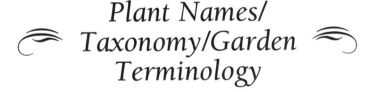

When we learn to call flowers by name we take the first step toward a real intimacy with them.
— MRS. WILLIAM STARR DANA, author of *How to Know the Wild Flowers: A Guide to the Names, Haunts, and Habits of Our Common Wild Flowers*, 1893

One of the least attractive expressions in the whole realm of gardening must be "plant materials." Landscape architects use it all the time. Of course they are in the business of creating effects, not breeding pansies or coaxing a wisteria to bloom, so perhaps they can be excused. But talk of "plant material" has always struck me as a bit insulting to the plants themselves. How would you like to be referred to as "human material?"

— CHARLES ELLIOTT, "Books," *Horticulture*, February 1996

How can roses with names like Space Invader and Electron presume to compete with the likes of Duchess de Montebello?

— CLARE ANSBERRY, "War of the Roses," *The Wall Street Journal*, July 1, 1991, comparing modern roses and old roses

. . . The old vernacular names [of flowers] are the connecting links between us and the flower lovers of all the ages—men, women, and children, a long line of them—stretching across the years through countless gardens, high and humble, through woods and meadows and marshes to the little gatherings of potent herbs and edible roots nestled against the protecting walls of ancient monasteries wherein were kept the first records of flowers and their names.

— LOUISE BEEBE WILDER, garden writer (1878–1938)

Many fine flowers are cursed with atrocious names. I'd just as soon call an iris "Cystitis" as to call it a name inspired by some gas-bag politician or some movie queen who wouldn't know her namesake's pistil from its stamens.

— JULIAN MEADE, *Bouquets and Bitters*, 1940

I don't mind "White Magic" or "Ivory Tower," but I shudder at "Snowflake," "Carpet of Snow," "Snowdrift," "Ice Queen," and "Glacier." Don't the companies realize their catalogs come out in January? No matter how unusual or how delightful these white bloomers may be, their names leave me cold.

— ROGER B. SWAIN, *Field Days*, 1983

I love being asked to identify plants, and I don't know which gives me more pleasure: to know what they are, or not to know what they are.

➤ ELIZABETH LAWRENCE, *Through the Garden Gate*, 1990

The Velvet Rose—what a combination of words! One almost suffocates in their soft depths, as though one sank into a bed of rose-petals, all thorns ideally stripped away.

➤ VITA SACKVILLE-WEST, *Some Flowers*, 1937

The jargon of any profession can be provoking to anyone who feels excluded by it. A botanical description is so packed with trade terms of Greek and Latin derivation that most gardeners feel repulsed. Yet the jargon is an essential shorthand to prevent it becoming impossibly long-winded.

➤ HUGH JOHNSON, *Hugh Johnson's Gardening Companion*, 1996

Everyone knows that one piece of a fern is a frond. Not everyone knows that one piece of bamboo is a culm, but now you do.

➤ DUANE CAMPBELL, *"Hortulan Wordplay," Green Prints* Winter 1997/1998

Taxonomists seem to love to mess with plant names. Now that plants can be identified right down to their chromosomes, many have turned out to be something other than they thought to be. Just when you get proud of yourself for remembering the name of sweet autumn clematis, *Clematis paniculata;* it gets changed to *C. maximowicziana,* and there has word that this plant may get another name change.

➤ KEN DRUSE, *The Collector's Garden*, 1996

Procumbens mortei, a Latin term describing certain plants which you still believe will revive when the season changes.

➤ JOSEPHINE SAXTON, *Down a Rabbit Hole*, 1996

It seems inevitable that in the matter of names there will always be a conflict of interest between botanists (who want to get it right) and gardeners (who want to get it right too, but to have it stay the same).

— CHARLES ELLIOT, "The Name Trade," *Horticulture*, January/February 1999

Once you start trying to do the right thing by plant names, you find that there are a great many that you have mispronounced all your life. Then your lot is not a happy one. For you must choose between continuing in the wrong and feeling very foolish. Having always said "ox-alice" and "pitt-osporum," I cannot now change to "ox'-alis" and "pittos'-porum" without a blush or a stammer.

— ELIZABETH LAWRENCE, "Camelias and Such," *Through the Garden Gate*, 1965

Drinks are a regular source of inspiration. There are "Chartreuse" (yet another *Kniphofia*); "Burgundy" and "Port Wine," both penstemons; a cotoneaster named "Pink Champagne" . . . *Pernettya mucronata* "Mulberry Wine" sounds chancy. If you don't want to risk a hangover, grow the rose called "Café" or the juniper "Mint Julep"—unless you prefer the Deep South version to the Arabian; but you will die of thirst if you rely on the tiny flowers of *viola odorata* "Skimmed Milk."

— JANE TAYLOR, "Today We Have the Naming of Plants," *Hortus*, Winter 1990

A great barrier seems to exist between the real plant lover and the mere dabbler in gardening. The barrier is formed by Latin names. The dabbler cannot be bothered with such names: a bellflower is a bellflower, a marigold is a marigold, and a spade is a spade.

— ROY C. ELLIOTT, *Alpine Gardening*, 1988

Our impressions of flowers are largely built up of broken multi-tudinous hintings, often exceedingly vague and indefinite, but by no means wholly arbitrary. It is from these dim suggestions that our ancestors have drawn our present names of flowers, sometimes with deep insight and poetic truth, sometimes with all sorts of flighty and fantastic colouring, lent by medicine, astrology or alchemy.

➤ FORBES WATSON, *Flowers and Gardens*, 1872

There is a rough and ready rule of thumb—as full of exceptions as a colander is full of holes—which is this: no syllable of a Latin name should be accentuated more than another syllable, unless it be unavoidable.

➤ ROY C. ELLIOTT, *Alpine Gardening*, 1988

It is absolutely useless to ask any gardener to spare you Latin names, for the excellent reason that nine out of ten alpine plants haven't got any English name.

➤ REGINALD FARRER, *My Rock-Garden*, 1908

I want to start an organization of embattled gardeners: The Society For the Prevention of Calling Daffodils "Daffies," Gladioli "Glads," Snapdragons "Snaps," Chrysanthemums "Mums." Latin at one end, cheap nicknames at the other; it's "Antirrhinums," or "Snaps." Never! A snapdragon is a snapdragon.

➤ JULIAN R. MEADE, *Bouquets and Bitters*, 1940

To give them their botanical names is to divest them of all magic. Reminiscing on frangipani-laden tropical evenings is evocative enough, and circumstances would seldom require the precision of *Plumeria acutifolia*-laden evenings.

➤ CHRISTOPHER LLOYD, *The Well-Tempered Garden*, 1970

Planting

Those that plant should make their ground fit [for rose trees] before they plant them, and not bury them in a hole like a dead dog.
  ← Seventeenth-century writer

Deciding where a plant goes is a complicated and trying business. A gardener can spend an entire day trying to get one plant in the ground, wandering around aimlessly, digging and refilling a number of holes. Like a dog that circles and circles to locate *the* spot to rest, my garden design is one part work and two parts walking around.
  ← THOMAS C. COOPER, "A Note from the Editor," *Horticulture*, June 1990

Plunkitis always leads to chaos.
  ← MARY ANN McGOVITY, *Taylor's Guide to Gardening*, 1987

Look for the sunny part of the yard. If that means putting your plants in the front, as opposed to the back, so be it. It might mean going to your neighbor's yard and asking for more space. This whole notion that all your gardening needs to be done according to some architect's code is nonsense.
  ← ROGER B. SWAIN, "Weekend Journal," *The Wall Street Journal*, April 9, 1999

It is not possible to use to any good effect all the plants that are to be had. In my own case I should wish to grow many more than just those I have, but if I do not find a place where my critical garden conscience approves of having any one plant I would rather be without it, than to endure the mild sense of guilt of having placed it where it neither does itself justice nor accords with its neighbours, and where it reproaches me every time I pass it.
  ← GERTRUDE JEKYLL, *Home and Garden*, 1900

Planting is the most nurturing act of the garden year. Holding a root ball in both hands, like a baby you're laying in a crib, is as deep and connecting a moment as gardening offers.

— PAT STONE, *Garden Design* magazine April/May 1995

It is an undertaking to be approached in a spirit of industrious fanaticism but easy reconcilement to failure; for whoever goes at it in a spirit of total seriousness can only end his career in one place—the insane asylum.

— WALTER B. HAYWARD, on trying to arrange planting for a full complement of blossoms, without clashing colors, *The Commuter's Garden*, 1914

An old way that farmers in the west of England and in parts of America judged whether their soil was ready for sowing in the spring was to go into the field, drop their pants, and sit bare-cheeked on the ground. If the earth felt warm to their buttocks it was ready.

— MONTAGU DON, *The Sensuous Garden*, 1997

All this planting, which I admit I can't resist—especially when I see ravishing things in other people's gardens which I haven't got and I long to have—has led to furious arguments. I firmly believe that more planting, particularly in corners, steep banks and awkward places which are difficult to keep, saves work. My husband is just as convinced it makes work. I say weeding needn't be done every week—mowing and tractoring does. So he is always cutting down my planting and I am always trying to reduce his mowing. As a result of these disagreements and of always being greeted by "Good God—not more plants," each time I returned home with some exciting shopping or even gifts from friends, I finally resorted to hiding everything under rugs or plastic bags or locking them in the boot of the car and only getting them out late at night, hoping they wouldn't be noticed until they were safely tucked into their new home.

— JOAN PAYNE, English gardener, 1987

Gardening is largely a question of mixing one sort of plant with another sort of plant, and of seeing how they marry happily together; and if you see that they don't marry happily, then you must hoick one of them out and be quite ruthless about it.

The true gardener must be brutal, and imaginative for the future.

→ VITA SACKVILLE-WEST, *A Joy of Gardening*, 1958

 *Plants*

You know as well as I do, my dear fellow, what professional gardeners are like when it is a question of moss. Moss for some obscure reason appears to infuriate them.

→ P. G. WODEHOUSE, *Leave it to Psmith*, 1923

I consider every plant hardy until I have killed it myself.

→ SIR PETER SMITHERS, noted Swiss plantsman, quoted in *The Collector's Garden* by Ken Druse

While there must still be wonderful and unknown plants in China, northern India, farthest South America, all awaiting discovery and fame, the vast floods of new introductions from those countries are certainly now over, except for a slight trickle of obscure rarities to satisfy the vanity of gardeners who refuse to grow anything that anyone else has. So if the geographical frontiers are becoming exhausted, an absolutely new and uncharted one is all around us: the past.

→ DAVID STUART and JAMES SUTHERLAND, *Plants from the Past: Old Flowers for New Gardens*, 1990

As every gardener knows this immobility of plants does not seem to be much of an impediment—they will arrive rapidly enough on any bare patch of soil.

→ ANTHONY HUXLEY, *Green Inheritance*, 1985

O, mickle is the powerful grace
that lies in herbs, plant,
stones, and their true qualities:
For nought so vile that on the earth doth live
But to the earth some special good doth give.
    ━ WILLIAM SHAKESPEARE, *Romeo and Juliet*, 1595

Plants, like people, are social or anti-social: the good plant has to be able to live amicably with other plants in the border.
    ━ RICHARDSON WRIGHT, *Greedy Gardeners*, 1955

A traveller should be a botanist, for in all views plants form the chief embellishment.
    ━ CHARLES DARWIN, naturalist (1809–1882)

By contenting itself with neglected corners of the earth, the yarrow gives us many valuable lessons on how to succeed.
    ━ NELTJE BLANCHAU, *Nature's Garden*, 1900

Plants are like people; they're all different and a little bit strange.
    ━ JOHN KEHOE, greenhouse foreman, Elizabeth Park Rose Garden, quoted in *Garden Smarts*, 1995

Each new plant is never thought of as a bauble or a prize, but rather as another piece of the puzzle. One by one, plant by plant, my understanding of the larger picture has grown, bringing into focus, an astounding, mind-boggling portrait of life on earth.
    ━ DAN HINKLEY, *The Explorer's Garden: Rare and Unusual Plants*, 1999

One of the best of graveyard plants.
    ━ SHIRLEY HIBBERD, on ivy, *Brambles and Bay Leaves*, 1872

Pretty they are not. But a garden can labor under a surfeit of prettiness, be too sweet or cheerful for its own good. Sometimes what's needed in the garden is a hint of vegetal menace, of nature run tropically, luxuriantly amuck. For this I recommend the castor bean.

➤ MICHAEL POLLAN, "Consider the Castor Bean," in *My Favorite Plant* by Jamaica Kincaid, 1998

Certain plants, like certain persons, are gifted with that indefinable quality which we call charm. Occasionally whole families are endowed with it and then how delightful it is to make their acquaintance one by one, recognizing in each some characteristic or grace that delights us!

➤ LOUISE BEEBER WILDER, *Adventures in a Suburban Garden*, 1931

My first hosta was the common variegated kind, "Undulata." It is tough as nails, divides easily, grows fast, but it sure is ugly. I don't know why anyone would ever buy another hosta after growing this dog.

➤ TONY AVENT, "Hostas," in *My Favorite Plant* by Jamaica Kincaid, 1998

Part of my personality does things on a grand scale. I can't have just one friend—everyone has something different to offer. It's the same with plants: one hosta doesn't say "hosta" to me. I want to know all their faces.

➤ WILLIAM BRINCKA, sculptor-gardener, Indiana, quoted in "By the Sculptor's Hand," by Carolyn Ulrich, *Horticulture*, May 1990

There is no maximum order.

➤ TONY AVENT, owner, The Plant Delights Nursery catalog, on hostas

The hardiness of plants fascinates us, perhaps because we sus-pect—rightly—that we shall never understand it. There is an air of mystery, of magic and jiggery-pokery, that surrounds hardiness. We can control aphids and mildews; we can profoundly influence the nutritional regime of plants. What we cannot do is say why a given plant, perfectly hardy in Acacia Avenue, is hopelessly tender in Sycamore Grove. The truth is that climate is too complicated and composed of too many variables for us to be able to categorize plants according to quanta of hardiness. This is why we experi-ment, and is the very foundation of the imperative that drives us to beat the local conventional wisdom concerning the hardiness of plants.

— JOHN KELLY, "Hardy Is as Hardy Does," *Hortus*, Autumn, 1990

Collectors thrill to tiny silver leaves or bronze ones, but little can excite the acquisition frenzy that leaves do with many colors at once.

— KEN DRUSE, on variegated foliage, *The Collector's Garden*, 1996

Making a garden out of variegates is difficult. There is the com-pulsion to collect every one without consideration of the effect overall. In the case of the coleus, it would be a jittery nightmare.

— KEN DRUSE, *The Collector's Garden*, 1996

They tell us that plants are perishable, soulless creatures that only man is immortal, but this, I think, is something that we know very nearly nothing about.

— JOHN MUIR, American naturalist (1838–1914)

⁀ *Pruning, Grafting* ⁀

Remember: no plant needs pruning; we prune for human, not horticultural, requirements.

— MONTAGU DON, *The Sensuous Garden*, 1997

In his wild-wood garden Jasper stayed late that evening, subduing and cutting into the thickets of encroaching briars. He very much enjoyed the work: delightful to slice below the woody knot from which the felons sprouted. It was a destruction of personal dislikes, and at the same time a ransom for objects to be considered precious.

— MOLLY KEANE, *Time after Time*, 1983

Lest you wish you never married him, refrain from speaking to a husband when he is in the midst of pruning a Climbing Rose. An hour among the thorns gives even the meekest man a thirst for blood. It boils his wrath up near the surface. The canny wife, finding him in this disposition, will set a long, cool drink nearby and go away quietly.

— RICHARDSON WRIGHT, *Another Gardener's Bed-Book*, 1933

Each tree should have the same cared-for appearance that a well-groomed horse presents in the satin shine of his coat.

— VISCOUNTESS WOLSELEY, *Gardens: Their Form and Design*, 1919

With cerebral application the French amputate their plants to the bare bones . . . born with the automation set to PRUNE.

— MIRABEL OSLER, *In the Eye of the Garden*, 1993

It's easy to be cavalier about clearing when "chain saw fever" strikes, but "oops" won't replace a tree mistakenly felled in haste.

— ANN LOVEJOY, *Gardening from Scratch*, 1998

Nothing is more miserable for the gardener, or uglier in the landscape than a garden laid out with clipped yews. . . . Without naming the most grotesque examples of the mutilation in England, it is clear that much beauty is lost in our gardens by the stupid and ignorant practice of cutting trees into unnatural shapes.
— WILLIAM ROBINSON, garden designer (1838–1935)

Good pruning is invisible. It looks as if everything grew to the right size and stopped.
— CASS TURNBULL, founder of Plant Amnesty, Seattle, an organization dedicated to teaching people how to prune their trees and shrubs correctly, quoted in *Horticulture*, August 1990

There is never exactly the right amount of garden. You have to be either increasing it by sowing, mulching and grafting or decreasing it by thinning out, cutting back and, of course, pruning.
— W. C. SELLAR and R. J. Y EASTMAN, *Garden Rubbish & Other Country Bumps*, 1937

A year or so ago, after a long and bitter relationship with an ancient wisteria that grew against the back of our house, I fell upon it with instruments of destruction—shovel, saw, lopping shears, and pickax—and, after the battle was over, replaced it with a row of demure and docile spireas. The strife between the wisteria and me had arisen from the fact that I am not a good pruner tending as I do to simply hack at branches that get in my way rather than scientifically and artistically shaping the subject. So I had felt more and more helpless as the old vine, knowing all the tricks took advantage of me.

. . . it surges blithely up from its grave under the spireas waving its lovely new apricot-tinted leaves about so beguilingly that I feel like a brute as I cut them down. I suppose this will go on forever unless I resort to Roundup. But listen to this: There's a new problem. I've just seen, in a nursery plant list, a double *dark violet-purple* wisteria—W. sinensis "Black Dragon." Good grief, I say to myself, is this going to start all over again?
— ELISABETH SHELDON, *The Flamboyant Garden*, 1997

Prune so the birds can fly through the tree in any direction.

— **Old farm wisdom**

If I'd had my way in this world, I'd outlaw electric trimmers. People get carried away. We have no glue to cement those limbs back on after they've erroneously taken them off. To preserve a natural look, you should avoid severe pruning.

— CY KLINKNER, **nursery worker, quoted in** *Garden Smarts*, **1995**

A combination of surgery and carpentry employed for turning a sow's ear into a silk purse . . . grafting is to gardening rather what dove-tailing is to woodworking: everybody's heard of it; most amateurs have a rough idea how it's done and some have had a go; but only the professional practises it as one of his normal, everyday skills.

— HUGH POPHAM, *Gentlemen Peasants: A Gardener's ABC*, 1968

Rain/Watering

Rain never falls when we want it, but it falls in the end, and if it did not there would be no gardens, no plants—no life at all.

— HUGH JOHNSON, *Hugh Johnson's Gardening Companion*, 1996

As the first norther of the season approaches, a great wall of thunderstorms moves in and drenches the earth. The soaking rains initiate a floral miracle peculiar to this region. Northerners search longingly for the first crocuses in the melting snow. Here it is rain lilies thrusting from crusted earth that bring special joy.

— SCOTT OGDEN, *Garden Bulbs for the South*, 1995

More and more I am coming to the conclusion that rain is a far more important consideration to gardens than sun, and that one of the lesser advantages that a gardener gains in life is his thorough enjoyment of a rainy day!
⟶ MARGARET WATERFIELD, *Flower Groupings in English, Scotch and Irish Gardens*, 1907

The Garden suffers from the long drought in this last week of July, though I water it faithfully. The sun burns so hot that the earth dries again in an hour, after the most thorough drenching I can give it. The patient flowers seem to be standing in hot ashes, with the air full of fire above them. The cool breeze from the sea flutters their drooping petals, but does not refresh them in the blazing noon. Outside the garden on the island slopes the baked turf cracks away from the heated ledges of rock, and all the pretty growths of Sorrel and Eyebright, Grasses and Crowfoot, Potentilla and Lion's-tongue, are crisp and dead. All things begin again to pine and suffer for the healing touch of rain.
⟶ CELIA THAXTER, *An Island Garden*, 1894

Above all, in your absence do not allow the children, the ignorant visitor, your husband, or your maiden aunt to play the hose on your poor defenseless plants.
⟶ ANNA GILMAN HILL, *The Bulletin of the Garden Club of America*, May 1929

The sky is darkening like a stain;
Something is going to fall like rain,
And it won't be flowers.
⟶ W. H. AUDEN, "The Witnesses," 1935

. . . last evening there was a gathering of grey cloud, and this ground of grey was traversed by those fast-travelling wisps of fleecy blackness that are the surest promise of near rain the sky can show. By bedtime rain was falling steadily, and in the night it came down on the roof in a small thunder of steady downpour. It was pleasant to wake from time to time and hear the welcome sound, and to know that the clogged leaves were being washed clean, and that their pores were once more drawing in the breath of life, and that the thirsty roots were drinking their fill. And now, in the morning, how good it is to see the brilliant light of the blessed summer day, always full of new life and abounding gladness; and to feel one's own thankfulness of heart, and that it is good to live, and all the more good to live in a garden.

— GERTRUDE JEKYLL, 1900

It will soon be clear that until it has been tamed, a hose is an extraordinarily evasive and dangerous beast, for it contorts itself . . . jumps . . . wriggles . . . makes puddles of water, and dives with delight into the mess it has made.

— KAREL CAPEK, *The Gardener's Year*, 1931

In terms of ease and evenness of application, nothing will ever match rain. Rain falls so evenly, wetting the lawn, the vegetable garden, the flower border, the fruit trees, and the forest. Downpours are such democratic events. If only we knew how to call them up. Scheduling a picnic, or starting to work on the roof sometimes does the job.

— ROGER B. SWAIN, *Groundwork: A Gardener's Ecology*, 1994

The watering of a garden requires as much judgment as the seasoning of a soup.

— MRS. HELENA RUTHERFORD ELY, *A Woman's Hardy Garden*, 1903

If constant sprinkling is needed, nature is clearly suggesting that an alternative would be better.

— HUGH JOHNSON, *Hugh Johnson's Gardening Companion*, 1996

Water makes a jungle; lack of it, a desert. Plenty of it makes one man a "born gardener" while another who shorts his garden on water wonders why he can't grow cucumbers and tomatoes the way they look in seed catalogs. The real secret of luxuriant gardens is plenty of water.

— RICHARD C. DAVIDS, *Garden Wizardry*, 1976

Weather means more when you have a garden: there's nothing like listening to a shower and thinking how it is soaking in around your lettuce and green beans.

＊ MARCELENE COX, *Ladies' Home Journal*, 1944

Expect rain if flies are biting more often and more severely than usual.

＊ Folk wisdom

No matter how cloudy the sky, it won't rain until you water your garden.

＊ TEXAS BIX BENDER, writer (1949–)

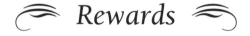 *Rewards*

There is peace in the garden. Peace and results.

＊ RUTH STOUT, *How to Have a Green Thumb Without an Aching Back* , 1955

The good gardener knows with absolute certainty that if he does his part, if he gives the labour, the love, and every aid that his knowledge of his craft, experience of the conditions of his place, and exercise of his personal wit can work together to suggest, that so surely will God give the increase. Then with the honestly-earned success comes the consciousness of encouragement to renewed effort, and, as it were, an echo of the gracious words, "Well done, good and faithful servant."

＊ GERTRUDE JEKYLL, *Wood and Garden*, 1899

My best compensation for my efforts is the words "You grew that yourself?"

— BONNIE MOSKOWITZ, Bayside, New York, passionate amateur award winner, *Garden Design* magazine, December 1995/ January 1996

A sharp flick, a steady pull, a gentle twist or a deep scoop—all are part of the relentless tactics of hand weeding. Only to another gardener could one admit to the foolish quickening of the pulse as one follows the tenacious root of a weed, the chagrin when it breaks off and the triumph when it pulls out whole.

— JILL PARKER, *The Purest of Pleasures*, 1988

Gardening gives me fun and health and knowledge. It gives me laughter and colour. It gives me pictures of almost incredible beauty.

— JOHN F. KENYON (1874–1959)

What greater delight is there than to behold the earth apparelled with plants as with a robe of imbroidered worke set with orient pearles and garnished with great diversitre of rare and costly jewels? . . . But these delights are in the outward senses—the principal delight is in the minde singularly enriched with the knowledge of these visible things, setting forth to us the invisible wisdome and admirable workmanship of almighte God.

— JOHN GERARD, *The Herball*, 1597

God Almighty first planted a garden: and indeed it is the purest of human pleasures. It is the greatest refreshment of the spirits of man; without which buildings and palaces are but gross handyworks: and a man shall eversee, that when ages grow to civility and elegancy, men come to build stately, sooner than to garden finely: as if gardening were the greater perfection.

— FRANCIS BACON, *Of Gardens*, 1625

Yes! In the poor man's garden grow,
Far more herbs and flowers, kind thoughts, contentment, peace of
   mind,
And joy for weary hours.
   ✐ MARY HOWITT

Is there a joy except gardening that asks so much, and gives so
much? I know of no other except, perhaps, the writing of a poem.
They are much alike, even in the amount of waste that has to be
accepted for the sake of the rare, chancy joy when all goes well.
   ✐ MAY SARTON, *Plant Dreaming Deep*, 1968

Personally, I feel both happier and more secure when I am reminded that I have the backing of something older and perhaps
more permanent than I am—the something I mean, which taught
the flower to count to five and the beetle to know that spots are
more pleasing if arranged in a definite order. Some of the most
important secrets are, they assure me, known to others than myself.
   ✐ JOSEPH WOOD KRUTCH, American naturalist (1893–1970)

Gardening has compensations out of all proportion to its goals. It
is creation in the pure sense.
   ✐ PHYLLIS MCGINLEY, "Against Gardens," *The Province of the
      Heart*, 1959

There has perhaps never been a time when we have more definitely
and more deeply needed our gardens. We are living in a queer,
spiritless time of confusion; there is very little sense of security in
life. We seemed to have lost our vision, to be filled with anxiety,
to feel that there is no long-distance view of life; and this is a
strange, bad negativeness, a chaos of the mind, than which there
is nothing more destructive. Perhaps one of the best ways to get
back to a sense of basic spiritual security is to work more and more
in the earth.
   ✐ CLARE LEIGHTON, garden writer, 1948

When I go into the garden with a spade, and dig a bed, I feel such exhiliration and health that I discover that I have been defrauding myself all this time in letting others do for me what I should have done with my own hands.

— RALPH WALDO EMERSON (1803–1882), "With My Own Hands"

A garden was one of the few things in prison that one could control. To plant a seed, watch it grow, to tend it and then harvest it, offered a simple but enduring satisfaction. The sense of being the custodian of this small patch of earth offered a small taste of freedom.

— NELSON MANDELA, **leader of the African National Congress that helped end apartheid in South Africa, spent 27 years in prison,** *Long Walk to Freedom,* **1994**

A garden isn't meant to be useful. It's for joy.

— RUMER GODDEN, *China Court,* 1961

A pleasant thing about gardening is that one may have for many years an intellectual awareness of diverse things, with certain vicarious pleasures, and then finally come to the actuality.

— B. Y. MORRISON, *The Bulletin of the Garden Club of America,* March 1940

Rock Gardens

Rock Garden. So named because it's perfect for busy people such as rock stars who travel a great deal and don't have time for nasty chores like weeding. All you need are a lot of large rocks, which will thrive in any climate and never need watering.

— MARTHA SMITH, *Beds I have Known: Confessions of a Passionate Amateur Gardener,* 1990

I have said that you should not use yellow for a dominant large patch close to the rocks . . . I feel that, as the earthquake caused the mountain, and storm has weathered it so that kindly Nature could soften it in places with life, storm and the colours of storm should run through the garden—purples, reds, bronzes, and deep blues, relieved by lighter tones, with occasionally a spot or thin streak (not a square patch) of yellow, like a fitful gleam of sun. These are the colours of the mountains. All other colours can be used restrainedly, but the predominant tones to use are the tones of the hills.

➤ H. B. SYMONS-JEUNE, *Natural Rock Gardening*, 1932

Times have wholly changed for the rock-garden. Fifty years ago it was merely the appendage of the large pleasure ground. In some odd corner or in some dank, tree-haunted hollow, you rigged up a dump of broken cement blocks, and added bits of stone and fragments of statuary. You called this "the Rockery," and proudly led your friends to see it and planted it all over with Periwinkle to hide the hollows in which your Alpines had died.

➤ REGINALD FARRER, *The Rock Garden*, 1912

From the early days of March until the cold of autumn descends, the rock garden will give us constant pleasure. A garden does not go from season to season, it goes from day to day. On our ability to choose our plants, to provide the right growing conditions, and to place them to the best advantage, will depend whether our rock gardens go from day to day, or whether—like a bed of daffodils—they become mere playthings of the passing season.

➤ ROY C. ELLIOTT, *Alpine Gardening*, 1988

Of all forms of cultivating flowers, rock-gardening is the most fascinating. Within a small space you may grow innumerable dainty plants, which would be swallowed up or would not thrive in the border—delicate Alpines, little creeping vines, cool mosses, rare orchids, and much of the minute and charming flora of the woods and mountains. Over this rock may trail the fragrant sprays of the twin-flower; here, at the base, a carpet of partridge-vine . . . and there a soldanella or Alpine gentian flash beside the fronds of an English fern. Then, its constant variety, and the inconceivable amount of plants it will contain!

    ← GEORGE H. ELLWANGER, *The Garden's Story*, 1889

There is something at once brilliant and useful about the Campanulas that takes the gardener's fancy almost more than the manifold admirable qualities of the gorgeous, incalculable Gentians, the easy-going but not dazzling little Saxifrages, or the striking, slug–beloved, rather capricious Primulas.

    ← REGINALD FARRER, *My Rock-Garden*, 1908

Roots

The first step in getting to know a plant intimately is to dig it up and study its root system. Learn how it eats and drinks. See how far it forages for food. Know your root, and garden wisdom will be added unto you.

    ← RICHARDSON WRIGHT, *Another Gardener's Bed-Book*, 1933

Nature does have manure and she does have roots as well as blossoms, and you can't have the manure and blame the roots for not being blossoms.

    ← BUCKMINSTER FULLER (1895–1983)

I don't wear gloves when hunting roots. A gloved rooter is as absurd as a blindfolded birder.

    ← SARA STEIN, on digging out weed roots, *My Weeds: A Gardener's Botany*, 1988

Seasons

In a garden . . . growth has its season. There are spring and summer, but there are also fall and winter. And then spring and summer again. As long as the roots are not severed, all is well and will be well.

— JERZY KOSINSKI, *Being There*, 1970

I am lucky to garden in a country with four distinct seasons and many variations in climate. Gardening is such an imperfect art that one is always thinking ahead to the next season, and there is never any guarantee that a harmonious grouping achieved one year will rematerialise the next. The complete change between midsummer greenery and winter's bare branches, with all the subtle differences in between, gives the gardener infinite scope for creating varied living pictures all through the year.

— JANE STERNDALE-BENNETT, "Winter at White Windows," *Hortus*, Winter 1993

Artificial and arbitrary division of a year into four unequal (and often indistinguishable) parts, expressly designed to baffle and mislead the gardener.

— HUGH POPHAM, *Gentlemen Peasants: A Gardener's ABC*, 1968

Some time after mid-March, one or more of the following significant events occur; Canada geese fly over, headed north; coldframes are left open all night; a snowdrop bayonet drops its head and opens; redwings, cowbirds, robins, starlings, grackles arrive; grosbeaks, juncos, red squirrels leave; a warm rain thaws the ground; the first windless 70° day since fall arrives; turkeys scratch the parking lot looking for leftover sunflower seed; raccoons quarrel after dark; chipmunks scrabble in the leaves looking for maple seed; hawks circle high overhead looking for food; the first seedlings sprout; the grass greens.

— GEOFFREY B CHARLESWORTH, *A Gardener Obsessed*, 1994

Spring

Queer things happen in the garden in May. Little faces forgotten appear, and plants thought to be dead suddenly wave a green hand to confound you.

━ W. E. JOHNS, "Trowel Work," *The New York Times Magazine*, May 15, 1949

Spring shows
What God can do
With a drab and dirty world.

━ VIRGIL A. KRAFT

April is one of those months that has four weeks but easily seven or eight personalities. You wake up one Saturday morning, say, and find the sun high and warm . . . and before you're done much work you break into a sweat and pull off your coat. Immediately, a cloud blows in from nowhere, the day turns from blue to gray; and a chill descends.

April is just that way: part June, part February.

━ THOMAS C. COOPER, "A Note from the Editor," *Horticulture*, April 1985

In the Spring of the year joy springs afresh in beholding the seeds, and young Grafts and plants spring forth vigorously and strongly. And the birds and blossoms breathing forth pretious and pleasant odours, rejoyce and delight the inward and outward senses, promising a plentiful harvest of fruits in autumne.

━ RALPH AUSTIN, *A Treatise of Fruit-Trees*, 1657

April prepared her green traffic light, and the world thinks "Go!"

━ CHRISTOPHER MORLEY, American poet (1890–1957)

Ere man is aware
That the Spring is here
The flowers have found it out.

━ Ancient Chinese saying

Hope, patience and work—these are the three graces of spring.

➤ RUTH SHAW ERNST, *The Naturalist's Garden,* 1987

April comes like an idiot, babbling and strewing flowers.

➤ EDNA ST. VINCENT MILLAY (1892–1950)

May and June. Soft syllables, gentle names for the two best months in the garden year: cool, misty mornings gently burned away with a warming spring sun, followed by breezy afternoons and chilly nights. The discussion of philosophy is over, it's time for work to begin.

➤ H. PETER LOEWER, *Month-by-Month Garden Almanac for Indoor & Outdoor Gardening,* 1983

There is nothing like the first hot days of spring when the gardener stops wondering if it's too soon to plant the dahlias and starts wondering if it's too late.

➤ HENRY MITCHELL, *The Essential Earthman,* 1981

Summer

Not until the advent of summer do the brilliant large flowers appear, the spring flora is smaller, more delicate, and generally more ephemeral. You must stoop down for the spring flower; the summer flowers reach up to you.

➤ GEORGE H. ELLWANGER, *The Garden's Story,* 1889

Any damn fool can have a garden in April and May. It separates the men from the boys when you've got an interesting place in August.

➤ ALLEN C. HASKELL, nursery worker, quoted in "Allen Haskell's Way," *Horticulture,* May 1991

The sound of summer is everywhere . . . a faint resonance seems to come from the very earth itself. The fervour of the sunbeams descending in a tidal flood rings on the strung harp of earth. It is this exquisite undertone, heard and yet unheard, which brings the mind into sweet accordance with the wonderful instrument of nature.

— RICHARD JEFFERIES, "The Pageant of Summer," *Longman's* magazine, June 1883

The awful shadow of some unseen Power
Floats though unseen among us,—visiting
This various world with as inconstant wing
As summer winds that creep from flower to flower.

— PERCY BYSSHE SHELLEY, "Hymn to Intellectual Beauty," 1816

On this day, summer, long wishing but not really sick receives her visitors with a certain deliberateness—a pretty girl who knows she doesn't need to stay in bed. The yellow squash illuminates the aging vine, the black-billed cuckoo taps out his hollow message in code (a series of three dots), and zinnias stand as firm and quiet as old valorous deeds.

— E. B. WHITE, American author (1899–1985)

Not a formal garden with the well-groomed beds
Growing scentless blossoms, waving haughty heads,
But a friendly tangle of the Columbine,
Hollyhock, and Roses, and Morning Glory vine.
Paths that lead to mazes of the growing things,
Guided by their perfumes, stirred by Robin's wings:
Rioting and twining without gardener's art,
Summer in my garden is summer in my heart.

— HUGH FINDLAY, *Garden Making and Keeping*, 1932

The summer world is the insect world. Like it or not, that is how it is. There are few insects that ever find the day too hot.

— DONALD CULROSS PEATTIE, botanist (1898–1954)

All the same, I cannot help hoping that the great ghostly barn-owl will sweep silently across a pale garden summer, in the twilight – the pale garden that I am now planting under the first flakes of snow.

— VITA SACKVILLE-WEST, *In Your Garden*, 1951

You'll know a real gardener at this season of the year by the fact that he keeps his hose busy and his hoe busy.

— RICHARDSON WRIGHT, *Another Gardener's Bed-Book*, 1933

What is one to say about June—the time of perfect young summer, the fulfillment of the promise of the earlier months, and with as yet no sign to remind one that its fresh young beauty will ever fade. The soft cooing of the wood-dove, the gladsong of many birds, the flitting of butterflies, the hum of all the winged people among the branches, the sweet earth-scents—all seem to say the same with an endless reiteration, never wearying because so gladsome. June is here—June is here; thank God for lovely June!

— GERTRUDE JEKYLL, *Wood and Garden*, 1899

Thinking about spring in August is like planning a new family at the age of sixty. The children are grown and out of the house and this is no time to start thinking about babies.

— CASSANDRA DANZ, *Mrs. Greenthumbs*, 1993, on the incongruity
of bulb catalogs arriving in August

Fall

There are two awakenings in the garden: one in spring, and one in autumn. But it is in autumn, when frost puts an end to the old year's bloom, that the garden year really begins; for then the pointed buds of the winter-flowering bulbs are breaking through the ground, and the buds of the wintersweet are beginning to swell. Soon afterward, stems of the Christmas-roses hump up, pulling the buds to the light, and when spring comes it finds winter flowers still in bloom.

— ELIZABETH LAWRENCE, *Gardens in Winter*, 1961

But now in September the garden has cooled, and with it my possessiveness. The sun warms my back instead of beating on my head. No longer blindingly bright, it throws things before me into sharp relief and deepening color. The harvest has dwindled, and I have grown apart from the intense midsummer relationship that brought it on.

➤ ROBERT FINCH, *Common Ground*, 1981

What more remains to say of the garden, now shorn of its beauty, except that each year one learns to love it more? Alone, defying frost and sleet, the tall blue monks-hood spires remain, to be stricken down in turn, and patiently await the dawn of spring.

➤ GEORGE H. ELLWANGER, *The Garden's Story*, 1889

Chinese Lanterns—the seed-cases of *Physalis franchetii*—are an autumn delight, and I am always happy to see them once more. Their papery fragility is part of their charm, and their bright colour gives a lift to an otherwise too-exquisite dried flower arrangement in too many subtleties of brown and beige.

➤ LYS DE BRAY, *Cottage Garden Year*, 1983

For the joys a garden brings are already going as they come. They are poignant. When the first apple falls with that tremendous thud, one of the big seasonal changes startles the heart. The swanlike peony suddenly lets all its petals fall in a snowy pile, and it is time to say goodbye until another June.

➤ MAY SARTON, *Plant Dreaming Deep*, 1968

October is nature's funeral month. Nature glories in death more than in life. The month of departure is more beautiful than the month of coming—October than May. Every green thing loves to die in bright colors.

➤ HENRY WARD BEECHER, American clergyman (1813–1887)

Winter

People who are not gardeners always say that the bare beds of winter are uninteresting; gardeners know better, and take even a certain pleasure in the neatness of the newly dug, bare, brown earth.

— VITA SACKVILLE-WEST, *How Does Your Garden Grow?*, 1935

Winter gardens are usually strong on evergreens and architecture, but both of these elements can be overdone to the garden's detriment. Architectural gardens that do not derive their character from plants are often lifeless.

— ANN LOVEJOY, *The American Mixed Border*, 1993

Most people, early in November, take last looks at their gardens, and are then prepared to ignore them until the spring. I am quite sure that a garden doesn't like to be ignored like this. It doesn't like to be covered in dust sheets as though it were an old room which you had shut up during the winter. Especially since a garden knows how gay and delightful it can be, even in the very frozen heart of the winter, if you only give it a chance.

— BEVERLEY NICHOLS, on winter-blooming flowers, *How Does Your Garden Grow?*, 1935

I prefer winter and fall, when you feel the bone structure in the landscape—the loneliness of it—the dead feeling of winter. Something waits beneath it—the whole story doesn't show.

— ANDREW WYETH, American painter (1917–)

Thank heaven for winter, when we can sit quietly and ease our aching knees and backs, with time to peruse seed lists, read, visit friends, write letters, and dream of yet more perfect gardens.

— H. LINCOLN FOSTER and LAURA LOUISE FOSTER, *Cuttings from a Rock Garden*, 1990

Despite March's windy reputation, winter isn't really blown away: it is washed away. It flows down all the kills, goes swirling down the valleys and spills out to sea. Like so many of this earth's elements, winter itself is soluble in water.

— ANONYMOUS

An important part in the winter landscape is played by the dead grasses and other herbaceous plants, especially by various members of the composite family, such as the asters, golden-rods, and sunflowers. Wreathed in snow or encased in ice, they present a singularly graceful and fantastic appearance. Or, perhaps, the slender stalks and branches armed with naked seed-pods trace intricate and delicate shadows on the smooth snow.

— MRS. WILLIAM STARR DANA, garden writer (1861–1952)

Go out by yourself, face the wind, hold up your head and thank God for this gardening year.

— RICHARDSON WRIGHT, *Another Gardener's Bed-Book*, 1933

To see one's urns, obelisks and waterfalls laid open; the nakedness of our beloved mistresses, the Naiads and the Dryads, exposed by that ruffian winter to universal observation; is a severity scarcely to be supported by the help of blazing hearths, chearful companions, and a bottle of the most grateful burgundy.

— WILLIAM SHENSTONE, unconnected thoughts on gardening,
  c. 1745

 *Seed/Propagation*

If all you want is a half dozen petunia plants, it is more economical to buy a flat of six seedlings raised by someone else than to buy 150 seeds for roughly the same price and spend three months rearing the plant yourself.

— ROGER B. SWAIN, *The Practical Gardener*, 1989

You're almost there, seed tray. You can make it. Push! Push! PUSH!
  ← PAT STONE, "Coaching Seedbirth," *Green Prints*, Spring 1999

After some thirty years, I still get a thrill watching seeds poke their green shoots up next to the kitchen or living room windows. That's one reason my husband and I start at least some of our seed indoors. When our care leads to healthy, vigorous adult plants, we can be justly proud of the harvest of fruits and flowers. Nature didn't do it all alone.
  ← RUTH PAGE, *Ruth Page's Gardening Journal*, 1989

If there is any living thing which might explain to us the mystery beyond this life, it should be seeds. We pour them curiously into the palm, dark as mystery, brown or gray as earth, bright sometimes with scarlet of those beads worked into Buddhist rosaries. We shake them there, gazing, but there is no answer to this knocking on the door. They will not tell where their life has gone, or if it is there, any more than the lips of the dead.
  ← DONALD CULROSS PEATTIE, *Flowering Earth*, 1939

Scatter ye seeds each passing year,
Sow amid winds and storms of rain,
Hope give the courage,
Faith cast out fear,
God will requite thee
With infinite grain.
  ← *Farmer's Almanac*, 1854

Propagation from seed is a matter of time, of not being in a hurry. You often have to wait two to three years for germination—some things have double dormancy. But you will get results, and to me the wait is worth it. I want to know a plant from A to Z. I like to see how a plant gets from here to there for myself.
  ← SUSAN DUMAINE, gardener-botanist, quoted in "Susan's Garden,"
  by John Barstow, *Horticulture*, April 1988

The seed waits for its garden or ground where it will be sown.
—— Zulu proverb

Fluffy-ruffle petunias are delicate plants. The seed is as expensive as gold dust and as fine. It take weeks to germinate. The seedlings must be nursed by hand. . . . Once brought months later to maturity, the huge multicolored blooms represent beauty flowered into life by the most desperate of measures.
—— MARJORIE KINNAN RAWLINGS, American author (1896–1953)

With regard to seeds—some look like snuff, others like very light blond nits, or shiny and blackish blood-red fleas without legs; some are flat like seals, others inflated like balls, others thin like needles; they are winged, prickly, downy, naked and hairy; big like cockroaches, and tiny like specks of dust. I tell you that every kind is different, and each is strange, life is complex.
—— KAREL CAPEK, *The Gardener's Year*, 1931

All the flowers of all the tomorrows are in the seeds of today.
—— Chinese proverb

We are living in a time of unrest and worry, but the same crocus will grow near the Black Sea as grows in Spain, and these flowers don't need passports and frontiers. The seed is beyond frontiers and beyond nationalities, and the growing of things and tilling the earth is one of the most international, one of the most unpolitical things we can possibly do. Don't ever forget that the seed is the most important thing in this whole world.
—— CLARE LEIGHTON, garden writer, 1948

I ask not for a larger garden,
But for finer seeds.
—— RUSSELL HERMAN CONWELL

Seeds are a unique way for plants to survive deadly cold and searing heat, months or even years of drought. Seeds are a way for plants, anchored to the same square foot of soil, to spread around the globe. Seeds of the dipper gourd, for instance, survive in salt water for a year—long enough for the gourds to drift across an ocean.

    — RICHARD C. DAVIDS, *Garden Wizardry*, 1976

And those seed packets, envelopes of promise they are, far too large for the salt-spoonful of seeds they contain, and yet scarcely large enough for the wonders they hold.

    — LESLEY GORDON, *Green Magic*, 1977

Senescence

There is a feeling of time passing in the air, a whiff of mortality that makes the last beautiful days of the gardening year all the more poignantly beautiful.

    — MONTAGU DON, *The Sensuous Garden*, 1997

The lily's withered chalice falls
Around its rod of dusty gold,
And from the beech-trees on the wold
The last wood-pigeon coos and calls

The gaudy leonine sunflower
Hangs black and barren on its stalk,
And down the windy garden walk
The dead leaves scatter,—hour by hour.

Pale privet-petals white as milk
Are blown into a snowy mass:
The roses lie upon the grass
Like little shreds of crimson silk.

    — OSCAR WILDE (1854–1900), "Le Jardin"

Gardens are meant to go to seed.
> ← JOHN McCLENNA, Ashintully Farm, Massachusetts, quoted in "Weekend Journal," *The Wall Street Journal*, July 16, 1999

To a gardener, life after death is a bottomless mystery, but one he accepts pretty much as a certainty . . . so that snow comes as a promise of new life ahead. Snow covers the failures of the past, too. The weedy corners are obliterated, the rough brown lawn is smooth and clean. Last year is forgotten. We look ahead. Next year is going to be better. We start planning for a year like nothing we ever knew before.
> ← RICHARD C. DAVIDS, *Garden Wizardry*, 1976

Every flower holds the mystery in its short cycle, and in the garden we are never far away from death, the fertilizing, good, *creative* death.
> ← MAY SARTON, *Journal of a Solitude*, 1973

A garden never knows when its over.
> ← PAULA DEITZ, quoted in *The Philadelphia Inquirer*, August 11, 1996

Sensual Gardening

While it is not obligatory to dabble your bare feet in the dirt to get the most out of your garden, it is a pity not to go barefoot at some time.
> ← MONTAGU DON, *The Sensuous Garden*, 1997

All talk of the pleasures of touch verges on and even transgresses into the world of eros.

It is no accident that Lady Chatterley's lover was a gardener.
> ← ALLEN LACY, *The Inviting Garden: Gardening for the Senses, Mind, and Spirit*, 1999

A place where nature is controlled to serve at, and for, human pleasure. If the jungle is a symbol of sex beyond human control, and the lawn a symbol of sex corseted and over-controlled, then the garden is a place where sex is available for human delight in a controllable context. Sexuality exists there within a framework of human civility much like the sensual drifts of Jekyll's plants within the framework of Lutyen's masonry . . . .

— ROBERT B. RILEY, professor of architecture and landscape architecture, quoted in *The Meaning of Gardens*, 1991

"Sex With Roses Can Be Fun"

— Title of an article by JOHN POTTSCHMIDT, an obstetrician, *The American Rose*, 1991

A flower's fragrance declares to all the world that it is fertile, available, and desirable, its sex organs oozing with nectar. Its smells reminds us in vestigial ways of fertility, vigor, life-force, all the optimism, expectancy and passionate bloom in youth. We inhale its ardent aroma and, no matter what our ages, we feel young and nubile in a world aflame with desire.

— DIANE ACKERMAN, *A Natural History of the Senses*, 1990

The greatest gift of a garden is the restoration of the five senses.

— HANNA RION, *Lets's Make a Flower Garden*, 1912

Sometimes I rose at dawn and stole into the garden while the heavy dew lay on the grass and flowers. Few know what joy it is to feel the roses pressing softly into the hand, or the beautiful motion of lilies as they sway in the morning breeze. Sometimes I caught an insect in the flower I was plucking, and I felt the faint noise of a pair of wings rubbed together in a sudden terror, as the little creatures became aware of a pressure from without.

— HELEN KELLER, *The Story of My Life*, 1982

How can one help shivering with delight when one's hot fingers close around the stem of a live flower, cool from the shade and stiff with newborn vigor!

━ Colette (1873–1954)

 *Shade*

There is nothing more agreeable in a garden than good shade, and without it a garden is nothing.

━ BATTY LANGLEY, *New Principles of Gardening*, 1982

There is a sense of luxuriance and mystery about plants growing in shade that you can never match in full sun. In shade, pale colors float like moths at dusk. In sun, they just look washed out. Despite this, many gardeners treat shade as a problem. Think of it instead as a heaven-sent opportunity: plenty of plants grow far better in shade than anywhere else.

━ ANNA PAVORD, *The Border Book*, 1994

The gardener with some shade, who combines the right plant with smart culture and appropriate design probably works a richer canvas than one who paints in unrelenting glare.

━ ROSALIE DAVIS, *Taylor's Guide to Shade Gardening*, 1994

Do not forget that "shade" does not mean total darkness under a greedy conifer, and that "half-shade" usually means something more like "more than half-sunny."

━ JOSEPHINE SAXTON, *Gardening Down a Rabbit Hole*, 1996

Shrubs

A garden without shrubs is like a stage without the star performers—all the props are there, as well as the supporting cast, but the main actors who give weight and substance to the play have not appeared.

— Reader's Digest, *Guide to Creative Gardening*, 1987

These shrubs with interlacing boughs, which limit my garden to but a little space, live upon a pleasant soil from which they gather hidden beauties of the centuries.

With the coming of the southland breezes in early spring there is a murmuring of soft colour which trembles into form and then these willful shrubs burst into a pageant of bloom.

— HUGH FINDLAY, *Garden Making and Keeping*, 1932

If you can't think of a specific reason for having a hedge, you probably don't need one.

— HARRISON L. FLINT, "The Four-Season Hedge," *Horticulture*, August 1985

My wife thinks I'm crazy running outside with my ruler, but I've measured the flowers at two inches. This plant's so vigorous it literally jumps out of its little root shoes, and the fluffy white bottle brush blooms are so fragrant they're like an open jar of honey.

— MICHAEL DIRR, professor of horticulture, University of Georgia, quoted in "Shrubs Chosen by the Experts," *The New York Times*, May 31, 1990, on the shrub Fothergilla Mount Airy

For this is one of the odours that carry us out of time into the abysses of the unbeginning past; if ever we lived on another ball of stone than this, it must be that there was box growing on it.

— OLIVER WENDELL HOLMES (1809–1894), on box

A shrub with a ten-foot soul is never going to look happy if it has constantly to be butchered to fit into a four-foot straightjacket.
— ANNA PAVORD, *The Border Book*, 1994

I have discovered rhododendrons, and my gardening friends don't know what to make of it. Rather like an interest in horse racing or having a son called Harry, this is traditionally a province of either the aristocracy or the vulgar classes, rarely of the tasteful middle ranks. We are interested in shrub roses and herbs, in muted colours and "architectural" things; not flowers the size of footballs in shades of Barbara Cartland pink.
— STEPHEN LACEY, "Stephen Lacey's Snippets," *Hortus*, 1989

Little houses are belted with bulging shrubs as mud rolls out from under a football.
— FLETCHER STEELE, landscape architect (1885–1971)

The meanest of all mean shrubs . . . dear to those to whom something growing with a fungus-like rapidity is a treasure.
— WILLIAM ROBINSON, garden designer (1838–1935) on *Ligustrum vulgare*, the common privet

Like a child with big feet, they seem destined to grow to a size proportionate to their large and noble flowers.
— ALICE M. COATS, on the magnolia, *Garden Shrubs and Their Histories*, 1964

Ninety percent of all home landscaping in the country today uses only some forty-odd species of woody plants, and that's a terrible thing to have to say.
— DR. J. C. RAULSON, professor of ornamental horticulture at North Carolina State University, quoted in *The Gardener's Eye and other essays*, 1992, by Allen Lacy

Soil

Unlike the weather, it can be improved.
— HUGH JOHNSON, *Hugh Johnson's Gardening Companion*, 1996

The perfect garden soil is a balanced mixture of five constituents: of solids perhaps two-thirds rock particles, of sizes ranging from small stones down to the tiniest specks of clay; one-third animal and vegetable matter, mainly dead and decayed but with a substantial population of living creatures; a considerable quantity of water and a remarkable amount of air. Unfortunately it is a rare occurrence for such a soil to form naturally.
— HUGH JOHNSON, *The Principles of Gardening*, 1996

Time spent preparing the soil is never time wasted. It's boring and you're not going to notice it when you're done, but it's the most important thing you can do. Remove all the existing weeds and rocks, and the more attention you spend adding organic material, the better. And don't walk on it when you're done!
— ROGER B. SWAIN, "Weekend Journal," *The Wall Street Journal*, April 9, 1999

During this coldest time of the year, the empty beds make me especially aware of a gardening constant: there is always more life below the soil surface than above it. Deep beneath my feet the soil remains a constant fifty-five degrees. 'Tis the season of root hairs, millipedes, grubs.
— JIM NOLLMAN, *Why We Garden*, 1994

It was not mine, I found, to coerce and to dictate, if I wanted to have a happy garden, I must ally myself with my soil, study and help it to the utmost, untiringly. . . . Always the soil must come first.
— MARION CRAN, "If I Were Beginning Again," *Gardens of Character*, 1940

Soil is our most valuable commodity. . . . Oil and precious elements we could do without, but we were born originally of the soil and must respect it. As a child I loved the feel and smell of soil and no doubt exasperated my mother by frequently being covered with it.

➤ BETH CHATTO, *The Damp Garden*, 1982

Feed the soil, not the plant.

➤ Old Amish saying

A rose in flower is, so to speak, only for dilettanti; the gardener's pleasure is deeper rooted, right in the womb of the soil. After his death the gardener does not become a butterfly, intoxicated by the perfumes of flowers, but a garden worm tasting all the dark, nitrogenous, and spicy delights of the soil.

➤ KAREL CAPEK, *The Gardener's Year*, 1931

Preserving topsoil means keeping it in place, and it means keeping the soil clean. Soil should never be treated as dirt.

➤ ROGER B. SWAIN, author of *Groundwork: A Gardener's Ecology*, 1994

The earth is nice and moist, crumbles beautifully in the fingers. . . . But that nice crumbly effect extends precisely one and one-fourth inches below the surface. Between seasons, somebody—probably a Foreign Power—has put in a concrete gun emplacement just under the topsoil.

➤ C. B. PALMER, "Memoir Written with a Non-Green Thumb, *The New York Times Magazine*, June 12, 1949

You couldn't raise an umbrella on that soil.

➤ Old folk saying

A good soil, like good food, must not be either too fat, or heavy, or cold, or wet, or dry, or greasy, or hard, or gritty, or raw; it ought to be like bread, like gingerbread, like a cake, like leavened dough; it should crumble, but not break into lumps; under the spade it ought to crack, but not to squelch; it must not make slabs, or blocks, or honeycombs, or dumplings; but when you turn it over with a full spade, it ought to breathe with pleasure and fall into a fine and puffy tilth. That is a tasty and edible soil, cultured and noble, deep and moist, permeable, breathing and soft—in short, a good soil is like good people, and as is well known there is nothing better in this vale of tears.

 ➤ KAREL CAPEK, *The Gardener's Year*, 1931

The pH value is one of the few instances in daily life where moderation is graphically praised . . . tell a gardener that his soil's pH is 14 or 0, he will keel over in a faint. Even 3 or 8 is very unpleasant to hear. No, a gardener cannot be pleased unless the number is greater than 5 and less than 7. 5 The middle terms are where fertility lies.

 ➤ WILLIAM BRYANT LOGAN, *Dirt: The Ecstatic Skin of the Earth*, 1995

Everyone agrees there are three basic types of soil—sandy, clay and loam. Making good garden soil is not a simple matter of combining the right proportions of these three ingredients. Building up soil is a matter of feel and smell and sight. A gardener tending the soil looks nothing like a lab technician for Dow Chemical; he's closer kin to a magician over a hat or a witch at a cauldron, for they are in the business of producing miracles from the most ordinary components.

 ➤ THOMAS C. COOPER, "A Note from the Editor," *Horticulture*, March 1988

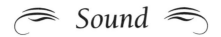

Sound

During summer months every garden is frantic with the busyness of insects gathering pollen, accompanied by a medley of hums, drones, buzzes and high-pitched sawing.
  ← MONTAGU DON, *The Sensuous Garden*, 1997

The temple bell stops
But I still hear the sound coming out of the flowers.
  ← BASHO (1644–1694)

What a pity flowers can utter no sound!—A singing rose, a whispering violet, a murmuring honeysuckle,—oh, what a rare and exquisite miracle would these be!
  ← HENRY WARD BEECHER, American clergyman, (1813–1887)

Steal out sometimes after sunset and walk up and down between the home end of the garden and the world end and listen to the sounds at each.
  ← RICHARD LE GALLIENNE, English poet (1866–1947)

Raindrops falling on parched soil at the end of the day are music to the gardener's ears.
  ← MONTAGU DON, *The Sensuous Garden*, 1997

Nine bean rows will I have there,
And a hive for the honey bee,
And live alone in the bee-loud glade.
  ← W. B. YEATS (1865–1939)

 Space/Size

The site of a garden has very little to do with its merit. It is merely an accident relating to the circumstances of the owner. It is the size of his heart and brain and goodwill that will make his garden either delightful or dull, as the case may be, and either leave it at the usual monotonous dead-level, or raise it, in whatever degree may be, towards that of a work of fine art.

— GERTRUDE JEKYLL, *Wood and Garden*, 1899

Don't try to till too much land. Better stick to what you can do well. It is of no use to spread time and labor and manure too thin. Concentration is wiser than expansion, just as union is strength.

— *The Old Farmer's Almanac*, 1922

Praise the large estate, but cultivate a small one.

— VIRGIL

How delightful to tumble head over teakettle in love with a beautiful tree, demure in its ten-gallon nursery bucket. However, it is imperative to ask the crucial question: How Big Will It Be? Practice saying that to yourself several times before you shop for trees; forget to ask and you can kiss your yard goodbye.

— ANN LOVEJOY, *The Year in Bloom: Gardening for All Seasons in the Pacific Northwest*, 1987

I plant enough tulips for the voles and me. With some problems I let nature take care of it. A few years ago I had a real rabbit problem. Now the rabbits are gone because the hawks are back. You do take your lumps with a garden of this size, but the advantage is that with most pest or disease problems, I can just go to a different part of the garden where it isn't happening.

— SUSAN DUMAINE, gardener-botanist, quoted in "Susan's Garden," by John Barstow, *Horticulture*, April 1988

I plant at least six times as much in a given yardage as will grow there. It's intellectually silly to be greedy, but still I am. If I can stick in one more thing, I will.

— HENRY MITCHELL quoted in "The Essential Earthman," by Barbara Seeber, *Horticulture*, April 1985

Planning a garden in a restricted place is tantamount to planning a small kitchen. It's much more difficult than laying out a big one.

— JOHN BROOKES, landscape designer (1933–)

With flowers, as with all other departments of the garden, you first decide what kind you want to grow and then whittle it down to what kind you can grow in the space. When you have further gone through the list and reduced it to what you can afford to grow and then eliminated the ones which you know from bitter experience will refuse to grow you have saved yourself a very great deal of labour indeed.

— ETHELIND FEARON, *The Reluctant Gardener*, 1952

It seems strange to me to write about a garden that is only 50 feet by 15 feet. But it extends upward and what it lacks in area is more than compensated by the joy that grows out of it and the uplifting and refreshment of the spirit of man.

— CELIA THAXTER, *An Island Garden*, 1894

A Garden should always look bigger than it really is.

— ALEXANDRE LE BLOND, *The Theory and Practice of Gardening*, 1712

Finding more space for more plants is a true test of ingenuity, more taxing than a jigsaw, and may well delay the onset of mental decay; it is impossible to stop thinking about this kind of problem until it is solved, at which point you discover another plant to crave.

— JOSEPHINE SAXTON, *Gardening Down a Rabbit Hole*, 1996

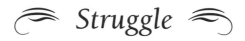 Struggle

"What of a drought?" says a voice. We answer, we keep doing and trust in Providence. Yes, we keep doing.
— *The Old Farmer's Almanac*, 1850

Your garden may appear to be a quiet place, but in reality it is an arena where hundreds of life-and-death dramas are played out everyday. Birth and death, killing and nurturing, even intrigue and cunning are all part of the complex community of life waiting to be discovered—and sometimes struggled with in your garden.
— ROSALIND CREASY, *Cooking from the Garden*, 1988

Gardeners are the ones who ruin after ruin get on with the high defiance of nature herself, creating, in the very face of her chaos and tornado, the bower of roses and the pride of irises.
— HENRY MITCHELL, garden writer (1923–1993)

It's a . . . torture rack, all that budding and pushing, the sap up the tree trunks, the weeds and the insects getting set to fight it out once again, the seeds trying to remember how the hell the DNA is supposed to go, all that competition for a little bit of nitrogen; Christ it's cruel.
— JOHN UPDIKE, American novelist (1932–)

Of course gardening is not for enjoyment. No, no, indeed not. It was never intended to be. There is no virtue in enjoyment. The hard grind, the solid slog, these are the character-forming attributes of our—I nearly said hobby—of our mission.
— CHRISTOPHER LLOYD, *In My Garden*, 1994

I am the fonder of my garden for the trouble it gives me.
— REGINALD FARRER (1880–1920)

 ## Sundial Mottoes

Come Light! Visit Me!
Light Rules Me
The Shadow, Thee
Time flies
There is no light without shade.
The sun shines for all.
The present is all you may claim as yours.
— ANONYMOUS

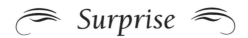 ## Surprise

One of the small delights of gardening, undramatic but recurring, is when phlox or columbines seed themselves in unplanned places. When trickles of creeping jenny soften stony outlines, or when Welsh poppies cram a corner with their brilliant cadmium yellow alongside the deep blue spires of Jacob's ladder, all arbitrarily seeding themselves like coloured smells about the place.
— MIRABEL OSLER, *A Gentle Plea for Chaos*, 1989

Nothing seems to me more surprising than the planting of a seed in the blank earth and the result thereof.
— CELIA THAXTER, *An Island Garden*, 1894

Pansies are continual surprises. I've used up a lot of film trying to capture faces with their different expressions.

━ CHARLIE GOODWIN, gardener, New York, quoted in *Horticulture*, February 1988

No year passes that one does not observe some charming combination of plants that one had not intentionally put together. Even though I am always trying to think of some such happy mixtures, others come of themselves.

━ GERTRUDE JEKYLL, *Home and Garden*, 1900

It is always a great pleasure—and surprise—when you happen on just the perfect place in which to plant some special treasure.

━ MARGERY FISH, *A Flower for Every Day*, 1965

❧ *Talking to Plants* ❧

I steadied my hand, knife poised for the incision. "Hello, I'm Judith, and I want us to work together to separate your root ball into two plants."

━ JUDITH HANDELSMAN, *Growing Myself*, 1996

The current fad for talking and singing to plants and telling them we love them will probably result in nothing more impressive than a vastly increased rate of plant mortality—as gardeners proceed farther and farther down the foolish road of what they presume to be utter communion.

━ HENRY MITCHELL, garden writer (1923–1993)

To get the best results you must talk to your vegetables.

━ PRINCE CHARLES, "Sayings of the Week," *The Observer*, September 28, 1986

I also strongly recommend discussing each problem out loud with yourself or with the patient (let's call it, rather than victim). Don't be put off by silly people telling you that talking to yourself is the first sign of madness. Pruning calls for concentration and if you talk over the intricacies of the task, it will pass off all the more smoothly.

— CHRISTOPHER LLOYD, *The Well-Tempered Garden*, 1997

As I work among my flowers, I find myself talking to them, reasoning and remonstrating with them, and adoring them as if they were human beings. Much laughter I provoke among my friends by so doing but that is of no consequence. We are on such good terms, my flowers and I!

— CELIA THAXTER, garden writer (1835–1895)

Instead of talking to your plants, if you yelled at them would they still grow? Only to be troubled and insecure?

— KATRINA NICKE of Walt Nicke Tools, Topsfield, Massachusetts, quoted in *Garden Prints*, Autumn 1998

 *Tools*

I have come to believe that the hose exists to try our characters. It tempers our distemper with humility and reminds us, I can't resist saying it, of the importance of going with the flow.

— JUDITH HANDELSMAN, *Growing Myself*, 1996

The most important tool a gardener can possess is a sense of humor. Keep it oiled, and not too sharp; you don't want to hurt yourself. Most important, keep it handy. You never know when you're going to need it.

— INEZ CASTOR, "The Most Important Tool," *Green Prints*, Summer 1995

There is a lovable quality about the actual tools. One feels so kindly to the thing that enables the hand to obey the brain. Moreover, one feels a good deal of respect for it; without it brain and hand would be helpless.

— GERTRUDE JEKYLL (1843–1932)

Spade! . . . Thou art a tool of honor in my hands;
I press thee, through a yielding soil, with pride.

— WILLIAM WORDSWORTH (1770–1850)

Notes are essential, because nothing is more easily forgotten than gardening resolutions.

— VITA SACKVILLE-WEST, *How Does Your Garden Grow?*, 1935

On mornings of determination I load the cart with an arsenal of gardening tools: loppers and pruners, rake, spade, fork and hand tools, as well as hoes. This is because weeding is like housecleaning. Cleaning reveals messes one hadn't known were there. The alternative to setting out with many tools is to set out with one, and one by one fetch all the others anyway.

— SARA STEIN, *My Weeds: A Gardener's Botany*, 1988

Gentlewomen if the ground be not too wet may doe themselves much good by kneeling upon a Cushion and weeding.

— WILLIAM COLES, *The Art of Simpling*, 1656

Choose well. This is the tool you'll use to show the earth, mother of all your molecules, how much you care.

— JEFF TAYLOR, "Love & the Trowel," *Garden Prints*, Autumn 1998

The plow is one of the most ancient and most valuable of man's inventions; but long before he existed the land was in fact regularly plowed, and still continues to be thus plowed by earthworms. It may be doubted whether there are many other animals which have played so important a part in the history of the world, as have these lowly organized creatures.

— CHARLES DARWIN, naturalist (1809–1882)

I'd had a lot of fun with that flame gun, it seemed the perfect answer to weeds, especially dandelions on the aforementioned terrace. In case you don't know, dandelions thrive on being burnt to the ground, they spring back redoubled in size and vigour overnight.

— JOSEPHINE SAXTON, *Gardening Down a Rabbit Hole*, 1996

Furthermore, if you have teenage sons, do not—I repeat DO NOT—allow them to do this part of the pest control for you.

— ANN LOVEJOY, *Gardening from Scratch*, 1998, **on using weed flamers**

Now sets do ask watering,
With pot or with dish,
New sown do not so if ye do as I wish:
Through cunning with dibble, rake, mattock and spade,
By line and by level, trim garden is made.

— TUSSER, *Five Hundredth Points of Good Husbandry*, 1573

Too many gadgets in the garden, as in the kitchen, are the sign of an amateur . . .

— JOSEPHINE SAXTON, *Gardening Down a Rabbit Hole*, 1996

 *Trees*

I have a particular feeling for this particular tree, and here is where the difficulty is. For I am about to kill it.

— BARBARA DEAN, "Hunting a Christmas Tree," *Green Prints*, Winter 1994/1995

A tree is a tree—how many more do you need to look at?

— RONALD REAGAN, **speech to the Western Wood Products Association, September 12, 1965**

I do not think anything in Nature is more mysterious or more effective than a big tree. . . . Standing under this one and looking up with knitted concentration, quite baffled, I got the impression that it emanated goodness. It stood there firmly like a noble thought, which if understood would save the world.

➤ JOHN STEWART COLLIS, *Trees*, 1989

Oh how sweet and pleasant is the fruit of those trees which a man hath planted and ordered with his owne hand, to gather it, and largely and freely to bestow and distribute it among his kindred and friends.

➤ RALPH AUSTIN, *A Treatise of Fruit-Trees*, 1653

A woodland in fall color is awesome as a forest fire, in magnitude at least, but a single tree is like a dancing tongue of flame to warm the heart.

➤ HAL BORLAND, *Sundial of the Seasons*, 1964

We shall go on planting trees, on into the future. We have the space and still have the energy, so they are a part of the garden which can be on-going in a way that increasing the number of flowers, roses and climbers would mean a long, serious think as to just what we can undertake. But trees are monuments. Once the decisions have been made, the roots spread out and compost laid, then you need only to stand back for sixty years. It has great charm that thought for gardens in the mind.

➤ MIRABEL OSLER, *A Gentle Plea for Chaos*, 1989

Plants are the young of the world, vessels of health and vigor, but they grope ever upward toward consciousness, the trees are imperfect men, and seem to bemoan their imprisonment, rooted to the ground.

➤ RALPH WALDO EMERSON, "Essays," 1844

Trees are the earth's endless effort to speak to the listening heaven.

➤ RABINDRANATH TAGORE, *Fireflies*, 1928

Sequoias, Kings of their race, growing close together like grass in a meadow, poised their brave domes and spires in the sky three hundred feet above the ferns and lilies that enameled the ground; towering serene through the long centuries, preaching God's forestry, fresh from heaven.

— JOHN MUIR, quoted in *Atlantic Monthly*, August 1897

Us sing and dance, make faces and give flower bouquets, trying to be loved. You ever notice that trees do everything to git attention we do, except walk?

— ALICE WALKER, *The Color Purple*, 1982

Woodman, spare that tree!
Touch not a single bough!
In youth it sheltered me,
And I'll protect it now.

— GEORGE POPE MORRIS, "Woodman, Spare That Tree," 1830

I think that I should never see a billboard lovely as a tree. Indeed, unless the billboards fall, I'll never see a tree at all.

— OGDEN NASH, *Song of the Open Road*, 1933

We tend to accept trees because they are there and because they take so long (we think) to grow. Yet a tree should have a reason for being there as much as any other plant.

— HUGH JOHNSON, *Hugh Johnson's Gardening Companion*, 1996

To plant trees is to give body and life to one's dreams of a better world.

— RUSSELL PAGE, *The Education of a Gardener*, 1962

When I look at the tree in the dark days of winter, its huge green-black skeleton silhouetted against the ashen sky, or hear its tracery seething in a westerly gale as I lie snug and warm in bed, I wonder who it was planted this giant for so many generations to enjoy. And in the balmy days of summer when its leaves are overlaid like the breast feathers of a great bird to form high domes of rounded foliage, I wish I could call back this gentle spirit of the past and say, "This is your tree. Look at it now, for it is gracious beyond words."

➤ NORMAN THELWELL, *A Plank Bridge by a Pool*, 1978

In the intimate and humanized landscape, trees become the greatest single element linking us visually and emotionally with our surroundings. Other manifestations of Nature—great rocks, deserts, moors, torrents, hurricanes—stir us, fill us with awe, make us afraid or humble, but a tree we understand and can allow to become part of us. It is no wonder that when we first think of a garden, we think of a tree.

➤ THOMAS CHURCH, *Gardens Are for People*, 1955

 *Vegetable Gardening*

They [flowers] were but garnishings, childish toys. . . . It was towards his cauliflowers and peas and cabbages that his heart grew warm. His preference for the more useful growth was such that cabbages were found invading the flower-plots, and an outpost of savoys was once discovered in the centre of the lawn.

➤ ROBERT LOUIS STEVENSON, *Memories and Portraits*, 1890

The act of putting into your mouth what the earth has grown is perhaps your most direct interaction with the earth.

➤ FRANCES MOORE LAPPE, *Diet for a Small Planet*, 1976

The smell of manure, of sun on foliage, of evaporating water rose to my head; two steps farther, and I could look down into the vegetable garden enclosed within its tall pale of reeds—rich chocolate earth studded emerald green, frothed with the white of cauliflowers, jewelled with the purple globes of eggplant and the scarlet wealth of tomatoes.

　━ DORIS LESSING, **English novelist (1914–)**

Sowe Carrets in your Gardens, and humbly praise God for them, as for a singular and great blessing.

　━ RICHARD GARDINER, *Profitable Instructions for the Manuring, Sowing and Planting of Kitchen Gardens*, **1599**

Our family hasn't tried to set any gardening records. We don't look for cabbages as big as beach balls or zucchinis as hefty as shillelaghs, we just want enough harvest to feed us. Let other gardeners seek immortality in the *Guinness Book of World Records*.

　━ RUTH PAGE, *Ruth Page's Gardening Journal*, **1989**

How do you feel about putting red chard in your flower garden? It is done, you know, and by the very best gardeners. I've seen ruby chard looking at its ease and as if sure of striking the right note in more than one purple-and-red border.

　. . . if you don't have a vegetable garden to put it in, you might perfectly legally grow it with your flowers. I would put leeks in my long border if I had the room.

　━ ELISABETH SHELDON, *The Flamboyant Garden*, **1997**

I want death to find me planting my cabbages.

　━ MICHEL EYQUEM DE MONTAIGNE, **French writer (1533–1592)**

I have often thought what a beautiful bit of summer gardening one could do, mainly planted with things usually grown in the kitchen garden only, and filling up spaces with quickly-grown flowering plants. For climbers there would be the Gourds and Marrows and Runner Beans; for splendour of port and beauty of foliage. Globe

Artichokes and Sea-kale, one of the grandest of blue-leaved plants. Horse-radish also makes handsome tufts of its vigorous deep-green leaves, and Rhubarb is one of the grandest of large-leaved plants. Or if the garden were in shape a double square, the further portion being given to vegetables, why not have a bold planting of these grand things as a division between the two, and behind then a nine-feet-high foliage-screen of Jerusalem Artichoke. This Artichoke, closely allied to our perennial Sunflowers, is also a capital thing for a partition screen; a bed of it two or three feet wide is a complete protection through the summer and to the latest autumn.
— GERTRUDE JEKYLL, 1900

Planted in the earth, eggplant looks homely. But put it in a container and a single plant can become the centerpiece of your garden. One plant can reward you with up to a dozen fruits, which is about all one family can eat without coming to dread the sight of them, in any disguise.
— JIM WILSON, *Landscaping with Container Plants*, 1990

If well managed, nothing is more beautiful than a kitchen-garden.
— WILLIAM COBBETT, *The English Gardener*, 1829

What shall I learn of beans or beans of me? I cherish them, I hoe them, early and late I have an eye to them; and this is my day's work. It is a fine broadleaf to look on. My auxiliaries are the dews and rains which water this dry soil, and what fertility is in the soil itself, which for the most part is lean and effete. My enemies are worms, cool days, and most of all woodchucks. The last have nibbled for me a quarter of an acre clean.
— HENRY DAVID THOREAU, *Walden,* 1854

Our vegetable garden is coming along well, with radishes and beans up, and we are less worried about revolution than we used to be.
— E. B. WHITE, American author (1899–1985)

There is a big difference between flowers you can eat and flowers you will enjoy eating. . . .

Chefs in fine restaurants are fond of edible flowers now, but I think that the fashion is destined to go the way of the hula hoop.

— JIM WILSON, *Landscaping with Container Plants*, 1990

Ripe vegetables were magic to me. Unharvested, the garden bristled with possibility. I would quicken at the sight of a ripe tomato, sounding its redness from deep amidst the undifferentiated green. To lift a bean plant's hood of heart-shaped leaves and discover a clutch of long slender pods hanging underneath could make me catch my breath. Cradling the globe of a cantaloupe warmed in the sun, or pulling orange spears straight from his sandy soil—these were the keenest of pleasures, and even today in the garden they're accessible to me, dulled only slightly by familiarity.

— MICHAEL POLLAN, *Second Nature*, 1991

Flowers, I have written, should be confined to a flower garden; but even there, they should form only the borders to long, rolling waves of sea-green cabbages and be interspersed with the purple pom-poms of the artichoke, with the knobs of onions and the scarlet flowers of the bean.

— OSBERT SITWELL, *Penny Foolish*, 1935

[Radishes] are the one amateur crop to be relied on. Many are sowed, but few are eaten, except those first prompt miraculous test cases which the gardener wipes on the seat of his overalls and eats on the spot, with no condiment but grit.

— BERTHA DAMON, *A Sense of Humus*, 1943

Training is everything. The peach was once a bitter almond; cauliflower is nothing but cabbage with a college education.

— MARK TWAIN, *Pudd'nhead Wilson*, 1894

To be an amateur vegetable gardener is to be spurred on by both artichokes that never appear and by summer squash that won't go away.

━ ROGER B. SWAIN, "Summer Squash," *Harrowsmith* magazine, 1986

The vegetable garden is red in tooth and claw. Tomatoes, red peppers, radishes, beets, plums and cherries span from vermillion through to ruby. It is worth planting ruby chard for entertainment value alone.

━ MONTAGU DON, *The Sensuous Garden*, 1997

I would rather sit on a pumpkin, and have it all to myself, then be crowded on a velvet cushion.

━ HENRY DAVID THOREAU (1817–1862)

As a mere vegetable or sauce as the country people call it, it does very well to qualify the effects of fat meat, or to assist in the swallowing of quantities of butter. There appears to be nothing unwholesome about it, and when the sort is good, it is preferred by many people to some other vegetables of the coarser kind . . .

━ WILLIAM COBBETT, *The English Gardener*, 1838, on the potato

If you value your time, consider carefully the extent of your vegetable garden, for what seemed initially an economic virtue can become a time-consuming vice.

━ JOHN BROOKES, *A Place in the Country*, 1984

Well, it never shows up in the United States Crop Reports, but a good estimate for the total harvest in any given year in our garden is eleven radishes, four tomatoes and a bent cucumber.

━ C. B. PALMER, "Memoir Written with a Non-Green Thumb," *The New York Times Magazine*, June 12, 1949

Cabbage, n. A familiar kitchen-garden vegetable about as large and wise as a man's head.

━ AMBROSE BIERCE, *The Devil's Dictionary*, 1911

Some things are a bad idea from the start.

➤ TIM RUTTEN, on growing iceberg lettuce, "This Year I Resolve," *Green Prints*, Winter 1993/1994

Pumpkins, I wonder at my need for them.

➤ LORNA MILNE, "Keepers of the Light," *Green Prints*, Summer 1998

By October, I am nauseated by the whole thing. I can hardly make myself can the final tomatoes and sauerkraut. I actively resent the squash and potatoes that must be brought in. . . ."I will *never* plant a garden again," I vow, as the last bucket of carrots disappears into the cellar.

➤ JEANNE DANIELSON, "Garden Fever," *Garden Prints*, Winter 1998/99

I hadn't subscribed to Ms. magazine for ten years only to end up sweating over kettles of boiling water.

➤ JANICE EMILY BOWERS, "Caught by the Canner," *Green Prints*, Summer 1994

Tomatoes

My journey to the gardener's paradise starts fresh each year on the third Saturday in February. That's the day I plant tomato seeds.

➤ JIM NOLLMAN, *Why We Garden*, 1994

People are growing tomatoes, at least in part, because it provides them with something to talk about. No other vegetable doubles as a social passport, no other vegetable makes it so easy for people of different ages, incomes, and educations to talk to one another. For many, just the subject of tomatoes is enough to leave a good taste in their mouths.

➤ ROGER B. SWAIN, *Field Days*, 1983

There's nothin' finer in life than true love and a home-grown tomato.

— GARY IBSEN, *The Great Tomato Book*, 1999

People who don't fish grow tomatoes. It gives them something to brag about. Tomatoes are better than trout in this regard, for in addition to size and number, there is the matter of earliness. Preseason trout, on the other hand, are illegal and not much discussed.

— ROGER SWAIN, *Field Days*, 1983

Zucchini

You run out of friends before you run out of zucchini.

— ANONYMOUS

Zucchini tend to hide their fruits under broad leaves until they have become monster green phallic clubs to mock all men and subvert the women.

— ARTHUR MILLER, "The Attractions of Gardening, After the Spring," *House & Garden* magazine, 1983

When one zuke serves 24, we're talking reckless gardening.

— WANDA FREEMAN, "Fed Up with Zukes: We're Not Going to Take It Anymore," *Detroit Free Press*, August 29, 1990

Each little girl carried her squash about in her arms and sang for it as for a babe.

— *Buffalo Bird Woman's Garden*: agriculture of the Hidatsa Indians [as told to] Gilbert L. Wilson, 1987

The giant marrow requiring wheelbarrow transport is cellulose in its most distasteful form.

— MILES HADFIELD, *The Gardener's Companion*, 1936

If you have mailboxes on your street, as we do on our Rural De-
livery, go around in the dead of night and stuff zucchini in the
boxes. I've done that.

← DONNA FUSS, gardener, quoted in *Garden Smarts*, 1995

There's something mysterious and wonderful—and well, incredi-
bly *fertile* about the Sicilian squash. And I contend that this plant
has a sense of humor. How else could it expose itself in such a
nonchalant, easygoing manner? Just dangling there, unaffected by
giggles or the questions of children.

← ANNE RAVER, *Deep in the Green*, 1995

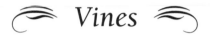 *Vines*

Of all plants, the climbers come the nearest to being human. A vine
seems to be endowed with intelligence and "the will to attain."

← MRS. STEPHEN F. CHADWICK, *The Bulletin of the Garden Club of
America*, February 1934

Orange climbers almost always look odd, like a zany traffic light.

← MONTAGU DON, *The Sensuous Garden*, 1997

When you have used up all your horizontal planting space, send
plants up to the sky, trained on trellises or wigwams, spread-eagled
on a wall, or lolling against the arches of a pergola. It is vital to
consider the scale and style of vertical features and how they will
fit in with the rest of the garden. A grand processional way through
a lushly planted pergola needs to lead somewhere more exciting
than the compost heap.

← ANNA PAVORD, *The Border Book*, 1994

It has been said that vines are to bits of architecture what a dress
is to a woman. It may serve to enhance beauty or to cover defects.

← LORING UNDERWOOD, *The Garden & its Accessories*, 1907

Some clematis will grow on a north-facing wall—but they will climb over the wall and flower for the neighbour. How generous are you?

— JOSEPHINE SAXTON, *Gardening Down a Rabbit Hole*, 1996

A doctor can bury his mistakes but an architect can only advise his clients to plant vines.

— FRANK LLOYD WRIGHT, architect (1867–1959)

We support a bill to make kudzu our national plant. Besides, what else smells sweet, tries to take over when you aren't looking, sneaks around through cracks and crevices, and does a wonderful job of covering its mistakes? No other plant more closely resembles our federal government!

— TONY AVENT, owner, The Plant Delights Nursery catalog

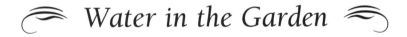

Water in the Garden

How often it is that a garden, beautiful though it be, will seem sad and dreary and lacking in one of its most gracious features, if it has no water.

— PIERRE HUSSON, *La Theorie et la Pratique Du Jardinage*, 1711

The water garden is an inspiration at any hour of the day. One always finds these water children of the bog-soil dressed in exquisite colours. Many of their stronger and taller relatives stand close to the edge of the pool as though they were interested in watching the velvet fingers of the breeze flake their trembling shadow spirits in the water.

— HUGH FINDLAY, *Garden Making and Keeping*, 1932

For Fountaines, they are a great Beauty, and Refreshment; But Pooles marre all, and make the Garden unwholsome, and full of Flies, and Frogs.

— FRANCIS BACON, "Of Gardens," an essay, 1602

The most relaxing of all places to be in a garden is by the side of a pond. That there should additionally be the sound of tinkling water seems quite unnecessary to me, but I may be in a minority. It merely irritates me to know that the tinkle depends on a circulating pump. Fountains have the further disadvantage of splashing your water lilies foliage, which they loathe. If you have a natural stream in your garden, that's different, but it is also unlikely and I, for one, don't want it.

— CHRISTOPHER LLOYD, *The Well-Chosen Garden*, 1984

One cannot praise the pond-lily; his best words mar it, like the insects that eat its petals: but he can contemplate it as it opens in the morning sun and distills such perfume, such purity, such snow of petal and such gold of anther, from the dark water and still darker ooze.

— JOHN BURROUGHS, American naturalist (1837–1921)

Weeds

What is a weed? A plant whose virtues have not been discovered.

— RALPH WALDO EMERSON, *Fortune of the Republic*, 1878

The process of weeding can be as beneficial to the gardener as to the garden. It gives scope to the aggressive instinct—what a satisfaction to pull up an enemy by the roots and throw him into a heap! And yet, paradoxically, weeding is the most peaceful of any outdoor task.

— BERTHA DAMON, *A Sense of Humus*, 1943

The sight of a good crop of weeds in a garden is not altogether an unwholesome sign. It certainly shows that the land is capable of something.
➤ WILLIAM F. ROWLES, *Every Man's Book of Garden Difficulties,* 1906

Don't treat weeding as a demeaning chore as vegetable and border people do. Weeding gives you the opportunity to get close to the plants.
➤ GEOFFREY B. CHARLESWORTH, *The Opinionated Gardener,* 1988

Weeding in a methodical way is most enjoyable, but if I have it in mind to tackle a certain area, I have to approach it with three-quarters-closed eyes (just wide enough not to walk into a pond or anything silly), otherwise I shall be distracted by other weeds or tidying jobs en route and shall never reach my destination.
➤ CHRISTOPHER LLOYD, *In My Garden,* 1994

It's difficult to weed too slowly though easy to go too fast. If you rush to clean an entire bed of anything—peas or peonies—you will end up nicking plants you set out to nurture. You will also miss the first signs of an aphid infestation or an outbreak of rust.

There is very little in gardening that benefits from being done quickly, and weeding teaches the virtues of pace as well as any activity.
➤ THOMAS C. COOPER, "A Note from the Editor," *Horticulture,* July 1988

Consider the intimate and curious acquaintance one makes with various kinds of weed—it will bear some iteration in the account, for there was no little iteration in the labor—disturbing their delicate organizations so ruthlessly, and making such invidious distinctions with his hoe, leveling whole ranks of one species, and sedulously cultivating another.
➤ HENRY DAVID THOREAU (1817–1862)

Because plants are part of the design of a garden and define its character they must be carefully chosen, but to look on them merely as garden furnishings would be to miss another whole world of pleasure, the different dimension that comes from learning about their place in the wider scheme of things, and from loving them for their own sakes—and not just the choicest kinds, but those that may not be considered garden-worthy, and even "weeds."

➵ Jo Munro, "A Sense of Place," *Hortus*, Autumn 1999

The weed of almost any month in this garden is the obnoxious, choking, smothering, detestable Ground Elder or Bishop Weed (*Aegopodium podagraria*). This hateful plant was introduced by the monks of long ago as a herbal remedy to soothe the pains of gout, and since gout was and is the result of a lifetime of tippling, those monasteries must have been quite cheerful places, . . .

➵ Lys de Bray, *Cottage Garden Year*, 1983

The fairest flowers o' the season
Are our carnations and streaked gillyvors,
Which some call nature's bastards.

➵ Shakespeare, *The Winter's Tale*, 1610–1611

Sweet flowers are slow and weeds make haste.

➵ William Shakespeare

Love of flowers and vegetables is not enough to make a good gardener. He must also hate weeds.

➵ Eugene P. Bertin (1921–)

There's only one sure way to tell the weeds from the vegetables. If you see anything growing, pull it up. If it grows again, it was a weed.

➵ Corey Ford, "Advice to the Home Gardener," *Look*, September 7, 1954

Be grateful for the weeds you have in your mind. Eventually they will enrich your practice. . . . We pull the weeds and bury them near the plant to give it nourishment.

— SHUNRYU SUZUKI, founder of the Zen Center at Green Gulch, "The Art of Zen Gardening," *Garden Design* magazine

Weeding is finicky work. It requires an overestimation of the importance of detail, a near-sighted view of things.

— SARA STEIN, *My Weeds: A Gardener's Botany*, 1988

Weeds have a peculiar fascination for us. They are endlessly interesting, like an enemy who occupies our thoughts and schemes so much more than any friend and who (though we would never admit it) we should miss if he suddenly moved away.

I know the weeds in my garden better than most of my flowers and, without them, my victories would be insipid affairs.

— URSULA BUCHAN, *The Pleasures of Gardening*, 1987

Now 'tis spring, and weeds are shallow-rooted;
Suffer them now and they'll o'ergrow the garden.

— WILLIAM SHAKESPEARE, *Henry IV*

How many a plant or flower is not doggedly uprooted, mowed or sprayed to death simply because it bears the name of weed, while another no better is patiently cultivated because the way has been semantically paved in its favor.

— PETER DE VRIES, "Reuben, Reuben," 1964

 Wildflowers

The beauty of woodland wildflowers is that they exist at all. Finding a painted trillium or a pink lady's slipper elicits exclamations of admiration, as much from surprise that such a delicate flower is thriving unattended as from an appreciation of its form and color.
— ROGER B. SWAIN, *Earthly Pleasures*, 1981

While June gardens are full of the masses of gaudy roses and daylilies we love so much, a more subtle show is going on in southern woods and fields. Millions of tiny white umbrellas make up the big white parasols of Queen Anne's Lace, in bloom now for nearly a month.
— WILLIAM LANIER HUNT, *Southern Gardens, Southern Gardening*, 1982

They won't bow to one's wishes. They don't want to be tamed. That must be the reason these darling, lovely little things won't cooperate.
— HELEN HAYES, actress (1900–1993), on wildflowers

May all your weeds be wildflowers.
— Gardening plaque

All you have to do to be a Wildflower Gardener is to amble out every week-end with a stick and a dog and note with approval, or in a bad season, with Contempt, the rather ramshackle results of Dame Nature's endeavours to do a bit of gardening on her own without reference to the Impossible Manuals.
— W. C. SELLAR and R. J. Y EASTMAN, *Garden Rubbish & Other Country Bumps*, 1937

The golden-rod is one of the fairy, magical flowers; it grows not up to seek human love amid the light of day, but to mark to the discerning what wealth lies hid in the secret caves of earth.

— MARGARET FULLER, *Journal*, 1840

Almost every person, from childhood, has been touched by the untamed beauty of wildflowers.

— LADY BIRD JOHNSON, founder, the National Wildflower Research Center

Women and Gardening

Millions of women between the ages of forty-five and fifty-five discover gardening. Other people imagine that this is because they have nothing else to do. In fact there is always something else to do, as every woman who gardens knows.

— GERMAINE GREER (1939–)

Gentlewomen these pleasures are the delights of leasure, which hath bred your love and liking to them, and although you are herein predominant, yet cannot they be barred from your beloved, who I doubt not, wil share with you in the delight as much as is fit.

— JOHN PARKINSON, *Paradisus in Sole, Paradisus Terrestris*, 1629

Usually the growth of greenstuff is checked by contact with a woman. Indeed, if she is also in the period of menstruation, she will kill the young produce merely by looking at it.

— DEMOCRITUS, fifth century B.C.

Lady, of so many sweet floures to chuse the best, it is harde, seeing they be all so good. If I shoulde preferre the fairest before the sweetest, you would happely imagine that either I were stopped in the nose, or wanton in the eyes: if the sweetnesse before the beauty, then would you gesse me eyther to live with savours, or to have made no judgement in colours: but to tell my minde (upon correction be it spoken) of all flowers, I love a faire woman.
— JOHN LYLY, *Euphues and His England*, 1916

The sanctity and reserve of these front yards of our grandmothers was somewhat emblematic of woman's life of that day: it was restricted, and narrowed to a small outlook and monotonous likeness to her neighbor's; but it was a life easily satisfied with small pleasures, and it was comely and sheltered and carefully kept, and pleasant to the home household; and these were no mean things.
— ALICE MORSE EARLE, garden writer (1851–1911)

Women who come to gardening only once their children have left home may find their horizons expanding in a way they never dreamt possible. Having given out to others in one way or another for years until they felt laid waste, they at last find a place of their own.
— MIRABEL OSLER, *A Breathe from Elsewhere*, 1998

Such was that happy garden-state,
While man there walked without a mate.
— ANDREW MARVELL, *The Garden*, 1681

LORD ILLINGWOTH: "The Book of Life begins with a man and a woman in a garden."
MRS. ALLONBY: "It ends with Revelations."
— OSCAR WILDE, *A Women of No Importance*, 1863

A man should never plant a garden larger than his wife can take care of.
— T. H. EVERETT, English horticulturist, author (1903–1986)

A gift of flowers to a woman implies that she is as deliciously desirable as the blossoms themselves; but there may be another and hidden message, contained in the old-fashioned phrases like "shy as a violet," "clinging vine," not originally conceived as pejoratives, that tells more of the truth—which is that flowers are also emblems of feminine submission.

— ELEANOR PERÉNYI, *Green Thoughts*, 1981

If I could only dig and plant myself! How much easier, besides being so fascinating, to make your own holes exactly where you want them and put in your plants exactly as you choose instead of giving orders that can only be half understood from the moment you depart from the lines laid down by that long piece of string!

I did one warm Sunday in last year's April during the servant's dinner hour . . . slink out with a spade and a rake and feverishly dig a little piece of ground and break it up and sow surreptitious ipomaea and run back very hot and guilty into the house and get into a chair and behind a book and look languid just in time to save my reputation.

— ELIZABETH VON ARMIN, *Elizabeth and Her German Garden*, 1898

Years ago, too, women,—always defined as ladies—plied outdoor tools in semi-shade, afraid of being considered vulgar or unfeminine; now the spade is recognized as an honourable implement in female hands.

— MARY HAMPDEN, *Every Woman's Flower Garden*, 1915

Index